MILNER CRAFT SERIES
Magic and Mystery
in
Cross Stitch

Robynn (Robynn-El) Milton

SALLY MILNER PUBLISHING

To my wild mum, Eenie R. C. B., Fairy Faye,
mystical Sue R. and Bernardine G.
Four beautiful goddesses who allow me to be me.
And to Lynne and Libby, in appreciation of
25 years of kept secrets.

First published in 1996 by
Sally Milner Publishing Pty Ltd
RMB 54 Burra Road
Burra Creek, NSW 2620
Australia

© Robynn L. Milton 1996

Design by Anna Warren
Photography by Ben Wrigley
Printed in Australia by Impact Printing, Melbourne

National Library of Australia
Cataloguing-in-Publication data

Milton, Robynn.
Magic and mystery in cross stitch

ISBN 1 863 186 5.
1. Cross-stitch - Patterns. I. Title. (Series: Milner craft series).
746.443041

Contents

Preface

My designs are based on legend and fantasy with a humorous or sometimes ecological poignancy.

'Leprechaun Gold' and 'Late Again ...' were designed for children and musicians respectively. Romance and tales of old are highlighted in '1589: The Crusader', 'Resting at the Castle Gates', 'Steeds in Flight' and 'Unicorn Lore'. 'Whale's Taile' and 'Dolphin Rainbow' were designed to keep us aware of the inherent beauty of our oceans. 'The Cherub' and 'Faery Council' will appeal to the child in all of us, as well as the romantic. 'Mystical ABC', the most complex of all my designs, highlights the magic and mystery that reveals truth really is stranger than fiction. From the angel to the blonde vampire with a conscience, the witch's black cat to the majestic lion, the scales of justice to the yin and yang symbol, this alphabet design incorporates myth, magic, legend, wishes and beauty that allow us to escape into a world where almost anything wonderful is possible. Join me.

Robynn-El

Introduction

⋆ ✦ ⋆ ✦ ⋆ ✦

Cross stitch appears in many traditional embroidery designs throughout the world. It is a very simple, effective stitch formed by two diagonal bars crossing at the centre and therefore can be used for outlines, borders, or to fill in an entire area. The basic cross stitch as implemented in this book is stitched in two parts — half the stitch is laid in one journey from left to right, then the top cross is stitched on the return. This ensures an even stitch tension, especially as all top threads lie in the same direction.

For each project a photograph, a chart, a colour key and a list of materials needed to make it is provided. Most of the charts are broken across two pages, with an overlap allowed on each page so that the charts can be photocopied then joined together. Arrows indicate the centre lines.

Thread numbers for DMC stranded cottons only are given, but confident stitchers can easily translate these numbers into another range of threads available on the market by using the colour names provided as further assistance to the reader.

I prefer to work with Aida 14 cloth, but Aida 18 would be suitable for a few of the designs, as long as the reader is aware that some of the designs in this book are for Advanced and creative stitchers and therefore involve intricate details and additional embellishments. If you use Aida 18 cloth the finished work would also be smaller and more difficult on the eyes.

Before stitching a design it is important for beginners to practise all stitches until they can produce them with ease.

Level of Difficulty

The projects in this book are graded with symbols next to their titles. The following is an explanation of these symbols:

***Beginner** – These designs involve full cross stitch and back stitch with basic tacking skills. (*'Late Again ...'* also includes four French knots.)

**Advanced – These designs may include overhand knots, three-quarter cross stitch, attaching beads and handmade tassels as well as full cross stitch and back stitch.

***Creative – *'Mystical ABC'* in its entirety requires extra patience and skill because of its intricate design and use of metallic threads, as well as all the techniques mentioned in the Advanced category. It is definitely worth the effort as an artistic project.

CHAPTER 1

Materials

- Aida 14 count in chosen colour – sold by the metre with a width of 110 cm (43 ½") or in fabric packs 30 cm x 45 cm (12" x 18")

- Tapestry needle size 24 or 26 (for evenweave fabrics)

- Pair of embroidery scissors

- DMC stranded cotton in nominated colours

- Metallic threads in gold and silver – these can be purchased from a craft outlet

- Frame— large floor tapestry stand with frame for *'Mystical ABC'* would be beneficial

- small embroidery hoop for individual letters

- lap frame for other designs

The following accessories will also come in handy:

- Lo-Ran Line Magnifier, Soft Ivory Magnetic Board (8" x 10"), Folding Stand – I place my design paper on the magnetic board which can be held upright in the folding stand. The line magnifier is a transparent and metallic ruler which allows you to keep your exact place on the graph and see the row underneath which you have already completed. These products allow for hands-free convenience for graphs and all pack flat for storage.

- Floss Box with cards to hold all your DMC threads

CHAPTER 2

Techniques and Stitches

Preparing Fabric for Stitching

Cut the fabric to the size stated, to allow at least 5 cm (2") of fabric around the design area for the frame. Overlock or oversew the edges of the Aida cloth, or use masking tape on raw edges to prevent fraying.

Sew a thread (in a different colour from your Aida cloth) horizontally and vertically on the fabric to show the centre. (The centre is marked on all diagrams on this book by tracking across the designs from the arrows on the edges of the design.)

It is best to begin stitching from the centre and work left to right. I tend to do the lower half of the design first so that when I roll the fabric around the frame to complete the top half, my work remains clean and dust-free.

Mount the fabric into the embroidery frame or hoop with the central stitch lying at the centre.

Stitches

I have employed the full cross stitch, three-quarter cross stitch, back stitch, straight stitch and a few French knots.

FULL CROSS STITCH

For a row of cross stitching, bring the needle up at the bottom left-hand corner (A), take it down at at B, bring it up at C, down at D and so on, until you need to turn. Now bring the needle up at K, down at H, up at I, down at F and so on, using the same holes as before.

For individual crosses or those on a slant, start at the lower left-hand corner of a square, bring the needle

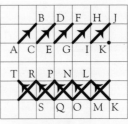

Cross stitch

9

through to the front, then down at the upper right corner, up at the lower right and down at the upper left (which makes one perfect cross). Then bring the needle up again at the lower left-hand corner of the next square.

THREE-QUARTER CROSS STITCH

These are useful stitches if you wish to avoid a sharp corner effect on a curve or for accentuating a pointed shape. When working two colours in the same square, ensure the main colour forms the three-quarter cross stitch and the subsidiary colour the quarter stitch. You need to utilise neatly the centre of each square to complete three-quarter and quarter cross stitches.

Work the first half of the cross stitch as per usual, but then take the second stitch down into the centre of the square, forming a 'quarter' stitch.

Three-quarter cross stitch

QUARTER CROSS STITCH

Work the quarter cross stitch into the centre of the square. Quarter stitches may begin from the left or right top corners and be worked down into the centre, or from the bottom left or right corners and up into the centre of the square. The rest of the square will either be filled up by a three-quarter cross stitch in another colour, or left blank until you outline the whole area.

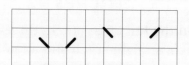

Quarter cross stitch,
to complement
three-quarter cross stitch

BACK STITCH

I have used back stitch for detailing and outlining shapes. To work back stitch, bring the needle up at A (holding a 1 cm, or 3/8", tail at the back, which you will secure by

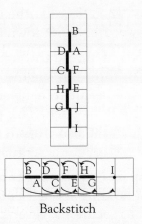

Backstitch

stitching over), down at B, up at C, down at D, up at E, down at F and so on. Each stitch goes through the hole twice.

STRAIGHT STITCH

Bring the needle up at A, down at B, up at C, down at D, up at E, down at F, up at G, down at H and so on.

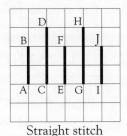

Straight stitch

FRENCH KNOTS

Bring the needle up at A (to the right of where you want the knot to lie) and wind the thread around the needle as shown. Hold the thread tightly while inserting needle back into fabric to the left of A. Pull the thread gently through to form the knot.

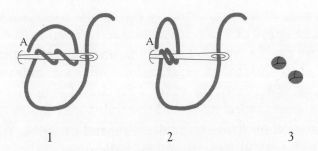

French knot

Hints for Working Cross Stitch

• Use two strands of thread throughout, unless otherwise stated. Cut thread in lengths of approximately 45 cm (18"). Allow the needle to hang and therefore the thread to untangle every so often. This prevents the thread looking thin, and it also stops it twisting in the fabric.

• Begin stitching by bringing the thread from underneath the work and holding about 1 cm (⅜") at the back. Work over this tail to secure it. Never knot.

• Always lay the first stitches in the same direction, that is, / / / / /, and lay the second stitches so that they cross over \ \ \ \ \ .

• To finish a colour, run the needle under about five stitches of the same colour at the back before snipping the thread.

• When using metallic thread such as gold or silver, work these stitches last for the full effect.

Care of Article

If you are using an embroidery hoop, remove your work from the hoop when you have finished a stitching session to prevent dirty marks or creases forming. If you are using a lap or floor frame, sew the Aida cloth to the framing material with wool.

While you are not stitching, cover the floor frame with a small cloth, or put the lap frame in a pillowcase. This will keep your work from becoming dusty or grubby.

When you have finished a project and you have checked all the stitches with a magnifying glass to ensure they are correct, you may wish to wash your work. I use mild soap or a wool wash in a bucket of lukewarm water. A slight spray of pre-wash stain remover can help to remove grubby marks. I dunk the work several times, leave it to soak for an hour and then flush it under cold running water until the water runs clear. Do not wring. Roll the wet fabric in a hand towel or towel to dry (depending on the size), gently blocking by hand. When dry, iron carefully on the wrong side.

Framing Suggestions

For an individual alphabet letter, you can choose an inexpensive Flexi hoop in your choice of colour from your local craft or a large department store. Follow these steps to neaten it on the back. Pad the inner space with three thin pieces of wadding or 1 thick piece cut to size, and fold over the edges of the fabric towards the middle and then glue those edges onto the back of the frame. Finally, glue a piece of stiff card (a little smaller than the frame) over it all for a neat, professional look.

For my other designs, I prefer to go to a professional framer or one of the many retail outlets where you can frame your own work with expert guidance at a reasonable cost. There is a wide choice of frames and colours, but it is best to choose a darker frame colour than the Aida cloth and also one that highlights one of the main colours.

Mounting boards cost more but set off your work beautifully. Never skimp on framing – you have put in many hours of skill and pleasure into your piece, so show it off to advantage.

Designs

Late Again ... *

Musical notes jet from this witch's magical broom as she hurries to her next engagement. The finished design measures 35 cm wide x 15 cm high (14" x 6").

Fabric:

Light blue Aida 14, approx. 45 cm x 25 cm (18" x 10")

Threads:

Symbol	DMC threads	Colour
/	333	dark mauve
o	550	rich purple
c	948	peachy cream
x	920	medium brown
••	221	red brown
▲	310	black

Techniques employed: *cross stitch, *back stitch and *French knots.

• Use 1 strand of black to outline witch's body and broomstick.

• Use 2 strands for musical notes (cross stitches and back stitches), rich purple city skyline, the words 'LATE AGAIN ...', and the witch and her broom.

• For greater definition, use 3 strands of black for shoes, eye, hat shadows and tie on broom.

To execute the musical notes, work one cross stitch at a time in the relevant colour, and back stitch around it before back stitching the stem of the note. Then proceed to the next note in that colour.

Leprechaun Gold *

The finished design measures 21 cm wide x 30 cm high (8 ¼" x 12").

Fabric:
Cream Aida 14, approx. 40 cm x 31 cm (15¾" x 12¼")

Threads:

Symbol	DMC thread	Colour
U	351	salmon
R	606	tomato red
4	722	pale orange
O	971	pumpkin
5	743	yellow
Y	972	gold
=	911	green
G	700	light forest green
<	996	light blue
B	995	intense blue
^	340	mauve blue
N	791	dark blue
2	210	pale mauve
P	208	dark mauve
/	954	pale green
C	738	sandstone cream
M	632	medium brown
X	413	dark grey
▲	310	black

You will also need a small packet of gold metallic stars (available from craft stores).

Techniques employed: *cross stitch, *back stitch and *tacking (stars).

• Use 2 strands for cross stitches.

• Use 1 strand of black to outline every item on leprechaun and pot.

There is no outline on the rainbow.

Finishing
Tack on the stars, following the blacked-out squares on the graph. I used 34 stars.

Attaching stars
'F' on ABC
Leprechaun Gold

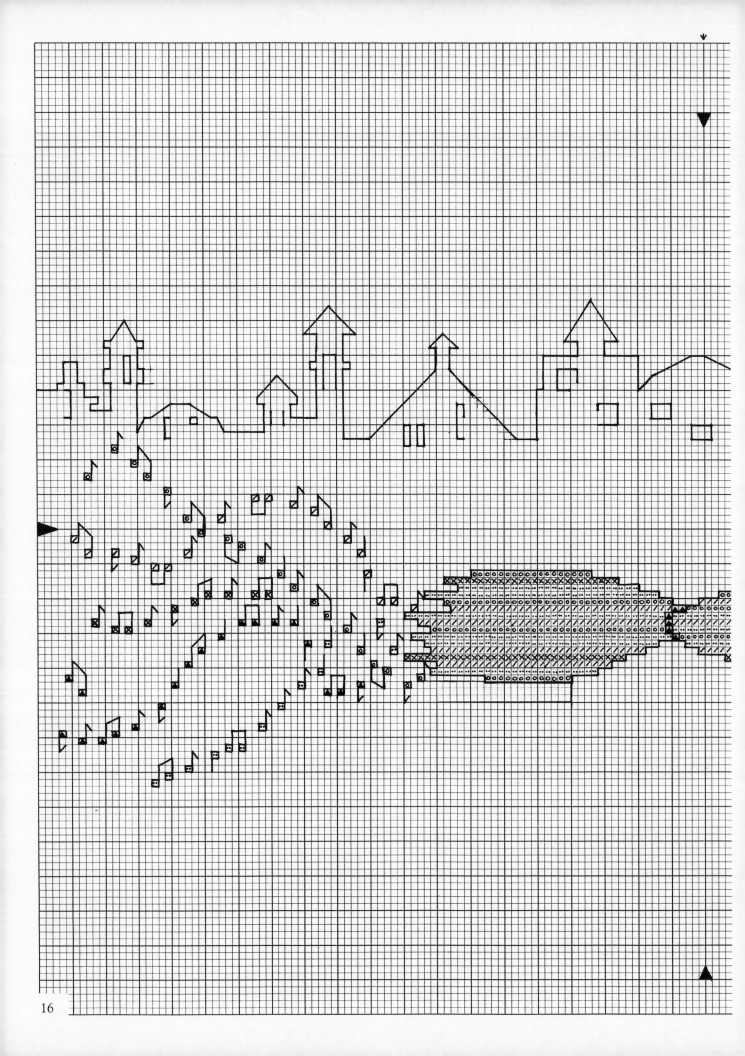

LATE AGAIN.....

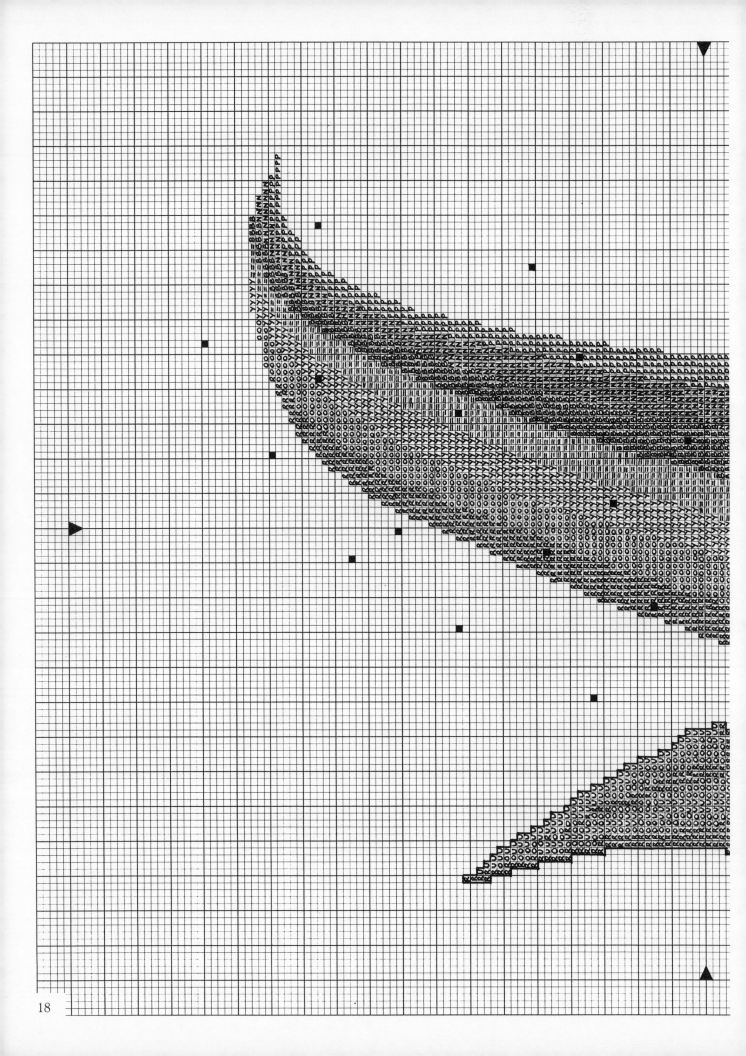

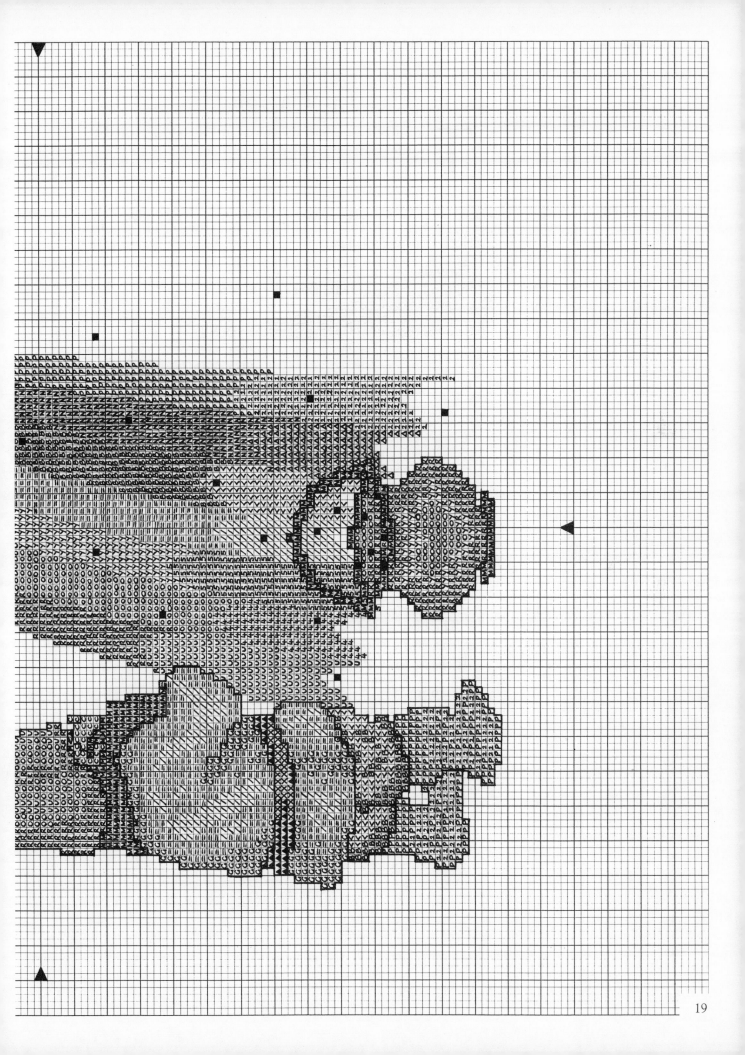

The Cherub **

The finished design, measured at the exterior of the border pattern, is 21 cm x 28.5 cm (8 ¼" x 11 ¼").

Fabric:

30 cm x 45 cm (12" x 18") piece of pale blue Aida 14 cloth (fabric pack size).

Threads:

Symbol	DMC thread	Colour
•	blanc	white
c	319	dark uniform green
<	356	light chestnut
2	407	grey chestnut
Y	741	dark yolk
=	945	orange cream
P	961	deep lolly pink
Δ	3685	burgundy cherry

Techniques used: *cross stitch *three-quarter cross stitch and* back stitch

* Use 2 strands throughout design, even for back stitch outlining.

* Outline arrow, shaft, hair, all body parts, wings and facial features with 3685.

* Outline green bow with same 319 green.

* The bow string is made from 2 strands 961 pink, with 2 long and 1 short (between chin and left arm) tacking stitches firmly at the back of the work.

Finishing

The border consists of 5 overlapping coloured lines in back stitch in a zigzag pattern. I began with dark yolk 741. For an even effect, work in 1 colour at a time so the layers of zigzag colour lying over each other is uniform all the way around.

Faery Council **

The finished design is 24 cm x 33 cm (9" x 13½") and leaves enough space for a border when it is framed.

Fabric:

30 cm x 45 cm (12" x 18") piece of cream Aida cloth (fabric pack size).

Threads:

Symbol	DMC thread	Colour
3	208	dark mauve
J	444	brilliant yellow
c	550	rich purple
Δ	554	pale purple
√	700	light forest green
n	718	bright deep pink
o	722	pale orange
*	902	rich brown burgundy
■	912	light apple green
e	915	deep pink
^	946	fluorescent orange
••	975	flat medium brown
7	3608	dark ice pink

Techniques used: *cross stitch *three-quarter cross stitch *back stitch *tacking (ties on vests)

• Use 2 strands throughout design, even for back stitch outlining.

• For a different effect, the fairies' skin is outlined in 975 only.

• There is no outline delineating the green stem.

• Outline body parts, wings, clothes, petals and skin ONLY when all the stitching around or behind the part to be outlined, has been completed in cross stitch.

• Outline the king's clothes, his wings and the queen's wings in 550 rich purple.

• Outline the green skirts, trousers, hats and the king's crown in 700 light forest green.

• Outline the petals, 4 vests, 3 fairies' wings (plus interior delineation), the king's collar, the queen's purple shirt and the purple sleeves of the 3 fairies in 902.

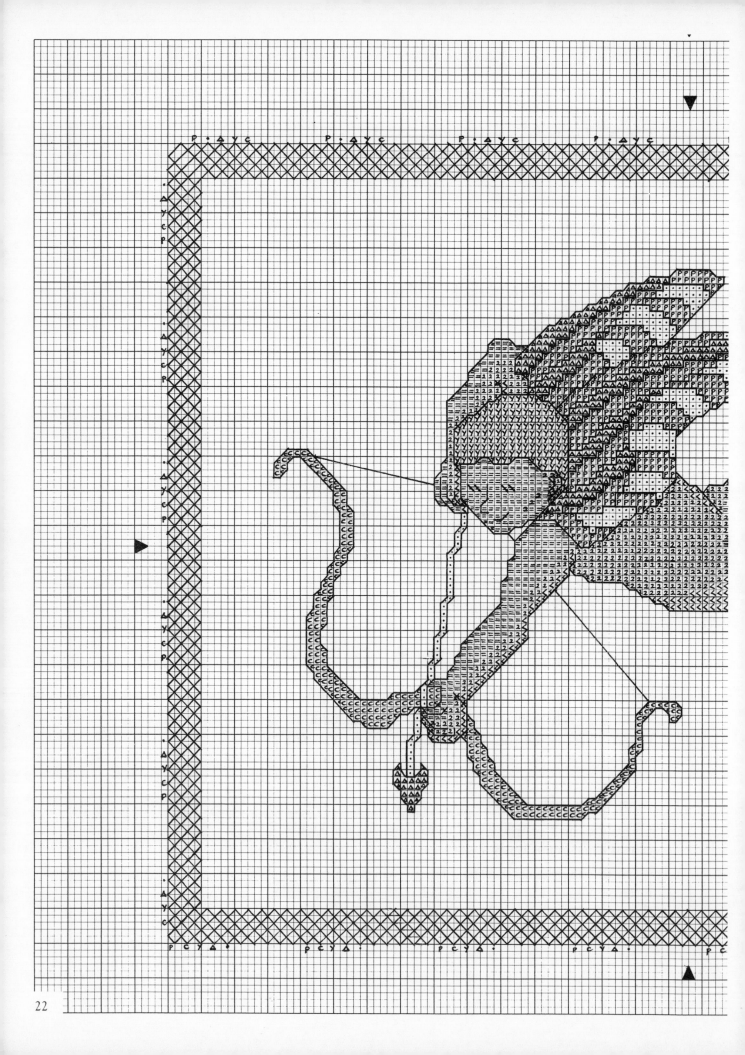

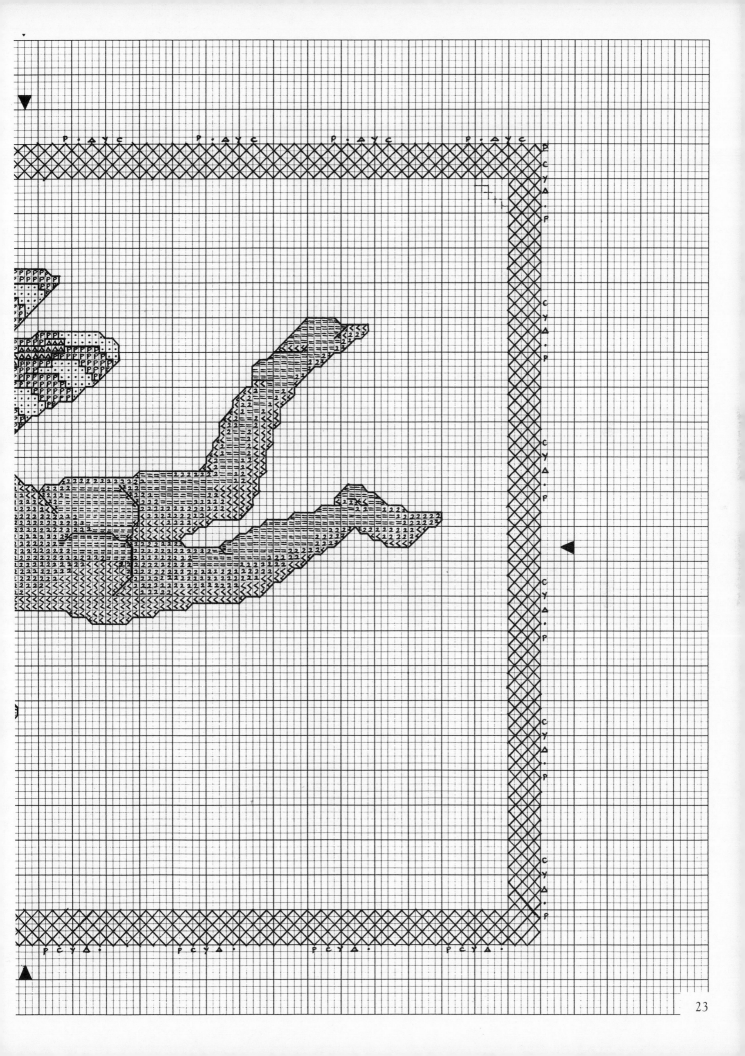

• The queen's antennae are stitched in back stitch in 700 green with 1 outlined cross at the end of each antenna.

• For the 8 buttons on the queen's vest and the 6 on the right fairy's vest, stitch each button in 444 bright yellow (when the rest of the vest has been completed) then outline each. To complete the tie attachment, tack between the inside top of each button to the adjoining button as shown on the graph.

• The bee is worked in 902 and 444 only.

• The bright yellow 444 stars on the king's collar are made with a large cross over the 902 stitching, then the vertical and horizontal bar laid over that, as per graph.

Unicorn Lore **

This design is based on the mythical unicorn, which had a red goatee beard and a tri-coloured spiralled horn in white, black and red.

The finished design measures 22 cm wide x 29 cm high (8½" x 11½").

Fabric:

Pale green Aida 14, approx. 40 cm x 32 cm (15¾" x 12¾")

Threads:

Symbol	DMC thread	Colour
•	blanc	white
▲	310	black
/	415	pale grey
x	414	grey
o	817	deep red
—	699	forest green
b	995	intense blue
••	–	metallic gold thread

Techniques used: *cross stitch, *three-quarter cross stitch and *back stitch.

• Use 2 strands for unicorn's body, red goatee whiskers, red hairs escaping from mane and tail, black skyline, green ground definition, and gold outlining of body (lower legs, back and top of tail) and horn.

• Use 1 strand of black for outlining neck, base of mane and tail, and hooves.

Finishing

For the unicorn's horn, cross stitch normally in the three colours (black, red and white). Then, using a double strand of gold thread, oversew in a slantwise direction from the base to the tip. I started at the bottom right, counted up 4 squares and put my needle across to the top left of that furthest left square, repeating this every row while advancing up one row at a time.

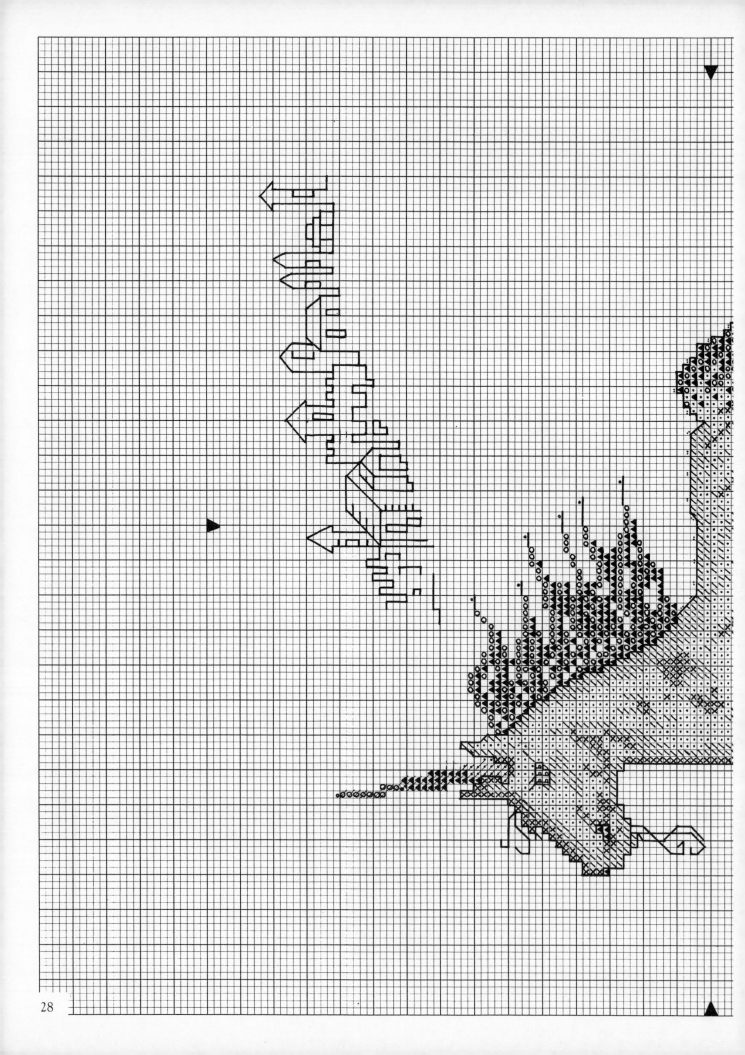

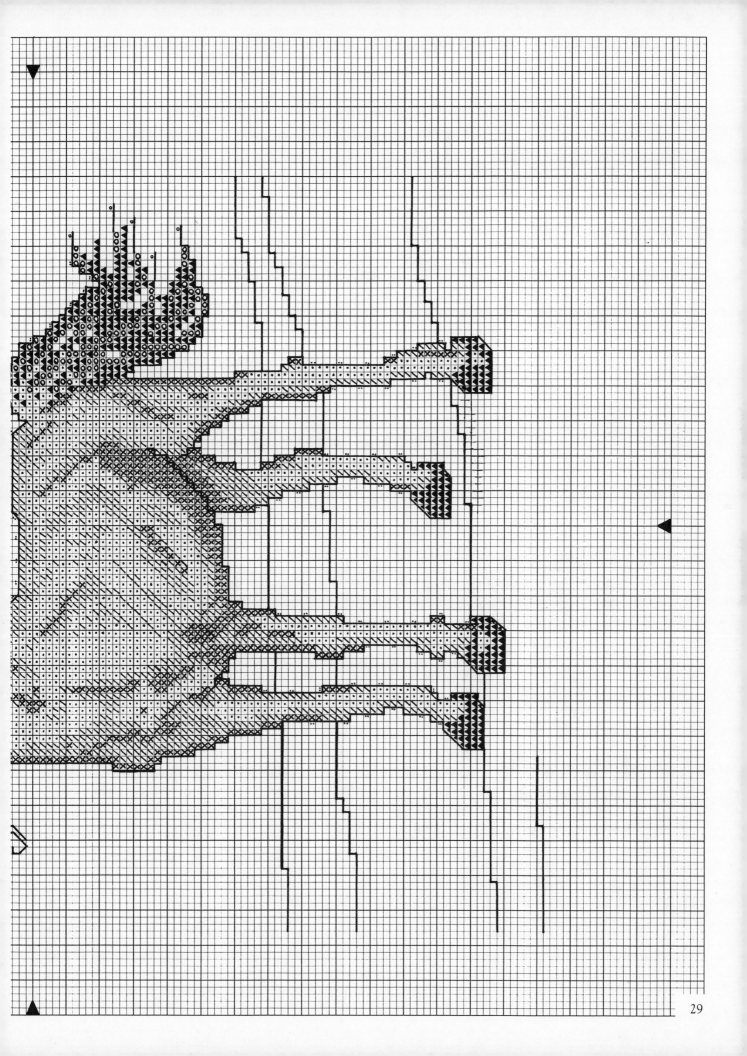

Resting at the Castle Gates **

The finished design measures 34 cm wide x 28 cm high (13½" x 11").

Fabric:
Cream Aida 14, approx. 38 cm x 44 cm (15" x 17½")

Threads:

Symbol	DMC thread	Colour
▲	310	black
/	743	yellow
=	972	gold
o	3340	salmon orange
J	943	jade green
P	605	pale pink
C	600	crimson
v	798	sea blue

You will also need small tubes of the smallest blue, green and red beads (available from craft stores) to bead the dragon's wings.

Techniques employed: *cross stitch and *back stitch.

• Use 1 strand of sea blue for mountains, 1 strand of jade green for tree silhouettes and outline of wings, and 1 strand of black for castle walls, teeth and total body outline.

• Use 2 strands of thread everywhere else.

Finishing

After you have washed and ironed the completed design, sew on the beads with yellow thread. Attach them as if you were sewing on a button with a shank. I randomly sewed the beads in each wing section to avoid a symmetrical pattern. From the top wing, working downwards, the dragon has 9 green beads, 36 red then 11 blue on the three darker wing sections, then 44 red, 33 blue, 29 green, 31 red, 22 blue, 14 green, 15 red and 9 blue on the lighter wing sections. Sew on the number of beads you are comfortable with.

Sewing on beads
1589: Crusader and
Resting at Castle Gates

1589: The Crusader **

The finished design measures 27 cm wide x 34 cm high (10¾" x 13½").

Fabric:
Light pink Aida 14, approx. 44 cm x 37 cm (17½" x 14½")

Threads:

Symbol	DMC thread	Colour
Y	973	bright yellow
o	740	orange
r	321	deep red
J	943	jade green
8	301	medium brown
U	801	dark brown
▲	310	black
4	794	light blue
■	796	royal blue
P	552	purple
•	415	pale grey
/	452	medium grey
X	317	slate grey

You will also need 9 small red beads (available from craft stores) for the reins.

Techniques used: *cross stitch, *three-quarter cross stitch, *back stitch and *overhand knot.

•	Use 2 strands for design, purple castle silhouette, black outline for the three hooves, and self-outline on red and purple dots on flag and shield.

•	Use 1 strand of black for the rest of outline.

Finishing
Oversew elongated crosses on the middle section of the lower jade and purple band of the horse's coat with a single strand of black.

Sew 9 red beads firmly on the blacked-out spaces on the purple reins.

Attach the 4 jade and 4 red tassels on the blacked-out squares on the horse's neck. Knot a complete skein (full 6 strands) on the wrong side of the fabric, leaving a small tail. Bring the strand through to the right side with your needle and knot it snugly next to the fabric twice.

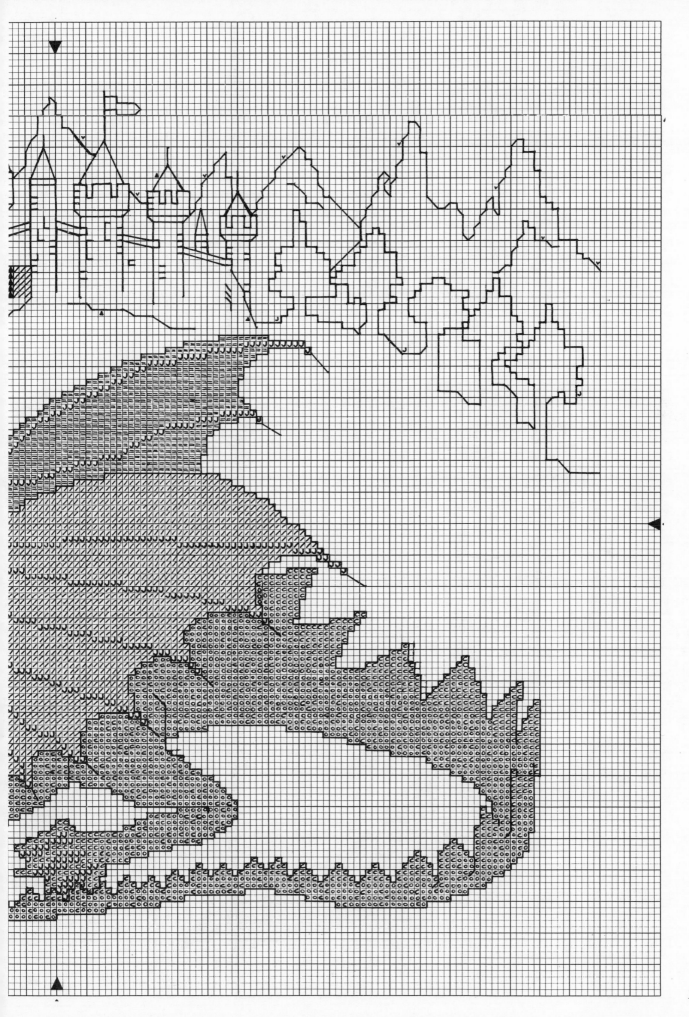

33

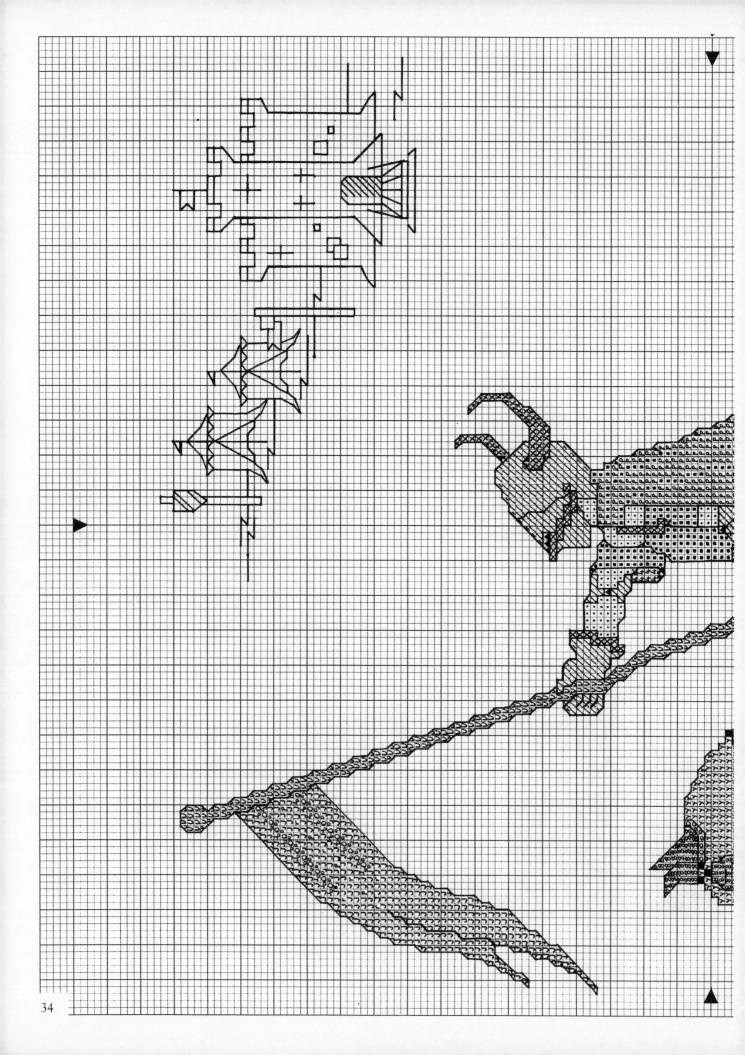

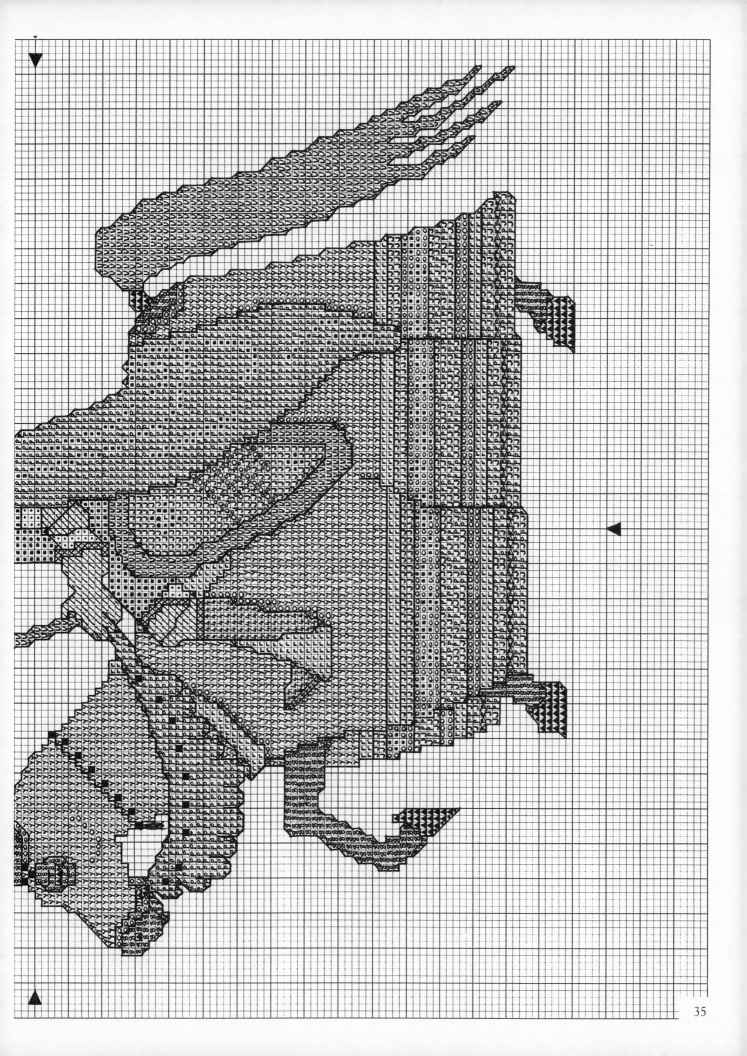

Cut the length to 1 cm (⅜").

Repeat this technique in black for the forelock. Place 3 knots under the left ear (on the blacked-out squares), brushing them towards the left like the flag, before cutting them slightly longer than the tassels.

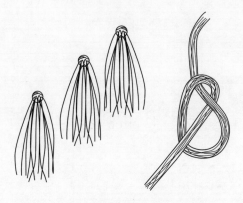

Tassels
(overhand knot) for
1589: Crusader

Whale's Taile **

In the dead of night, a whale surfaces in the moonlight and is caught by the artist before it crashes to the depths of the ocean again.

This design requires extra patience because of the use of three-quarter cross stitches and the dark colour of the fabric. Use a pale pink mounting board and navy frame to highlight the colours used.

The finished design measures 32 cm wide x 18 cm high (12¾" x 7").

Fabric:
Navy Aida 14, approx. 42 cm x 28 cm (16 ½" x 11")

Threads:

Symbol	DMC thread	Colour
/	blanc	white
P	963	pale pink
r	318	light grey
s	813	pale blue
Δ	517	medium blue
x	796	royal blue

Techniques employed: *cross stitch, *three-quarter cross stitch and *back stitch.

• Use 2 strands of thread throughout the design. Outline tail and shadow with 2 strands of royal blue.

Note that there is no outline around the individual water marks and ripples. The blank spaces in the reflection of the tail on the water hint at gaps caused by the moonlight.

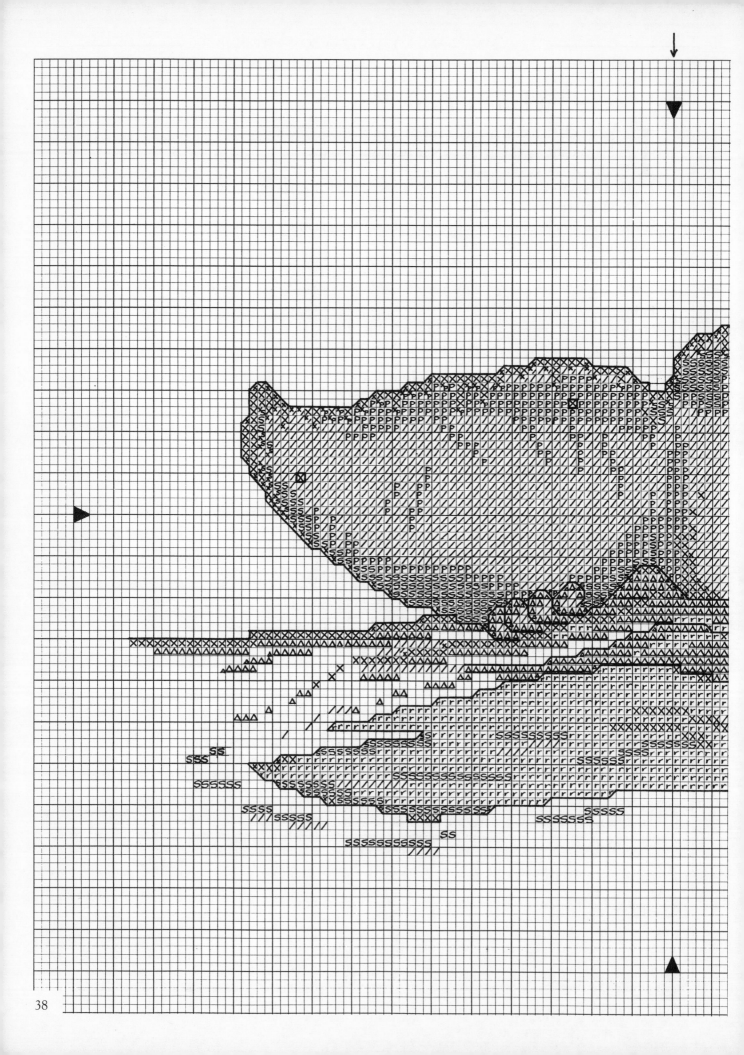

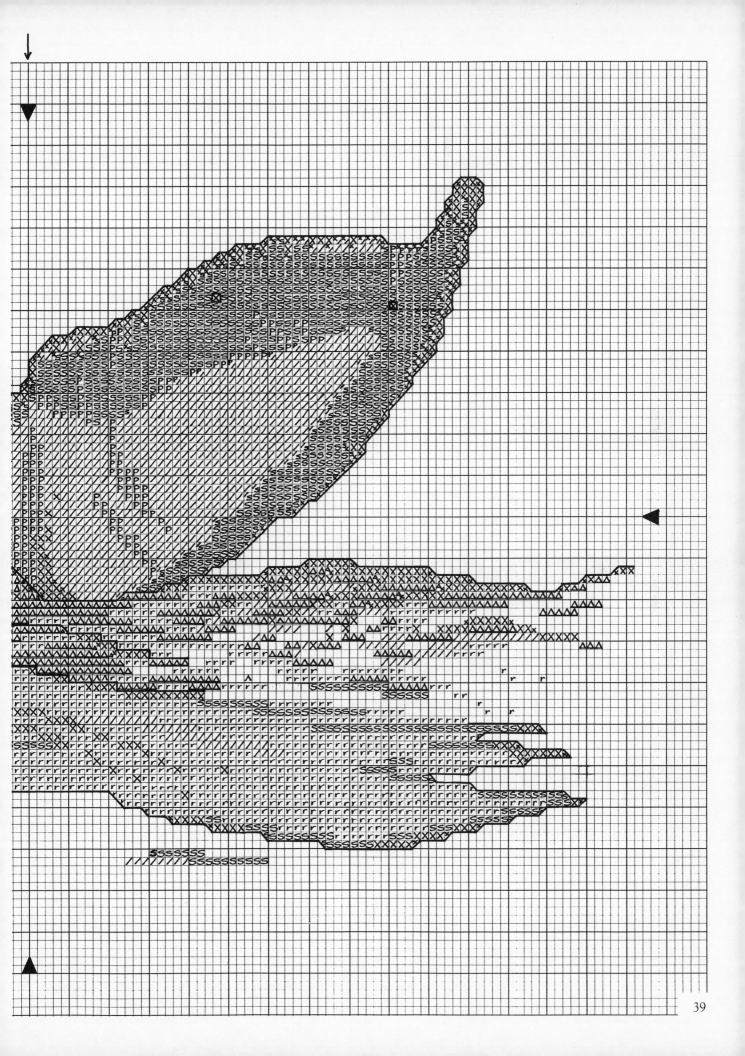

Dolphin Rainbow **

The round frame maintains the flow of this design. The finished design measures 26 cm (10 ¼") in diameter.

Fabric:
Pale blue Aida 14, approx. 35 cm (14") square

Threads:

Symbol	DMC thread	Colour
▲	310	black
•	762	light grey
/	318	blue grey
X	413	dark grey
U	891	dark pink
R	666	red
4	722	pale orange
O	608	orange
5	745	pale yellow
Y	307	fluoro yellow
=	703	light green
G	904	pea green
<	996	light blue
B	995	intense blue
Δ	798	sea blue
N	336	navy
2	209	mauve
P	552	purple

Techniques employed: *cross stitch, *three-quarter cross stitch and *back stitch.

• Use 2 strands for cross stitches, and for definition use 2 strands of black to outline the dolphins' foremost body parts – their eyes, mouth and jaw, and the shadowed parts of their fins.

• Use 1 strand of black to outline the six dolphins.

THE CHERUB

LATE AGAIN...

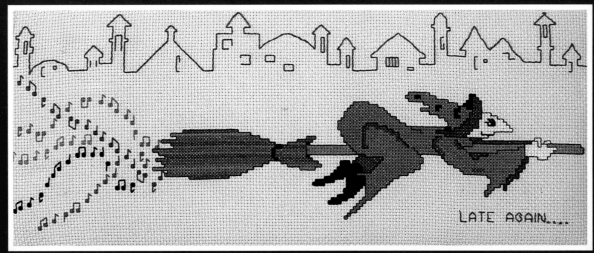

FAERY COUNCIL

LEPRECHAUN GOLD

UNICORN LORE

Robynn-El

RESTING AT THE CASTLE GATES

1589: THE CRUSADER

WHALE'S TAILE

DOLPHIN RAINBOW

STEEDS IN FLIGHT

In the beginning there was the......

and in the end

there was still

the magic.

MYSTICAL ABC

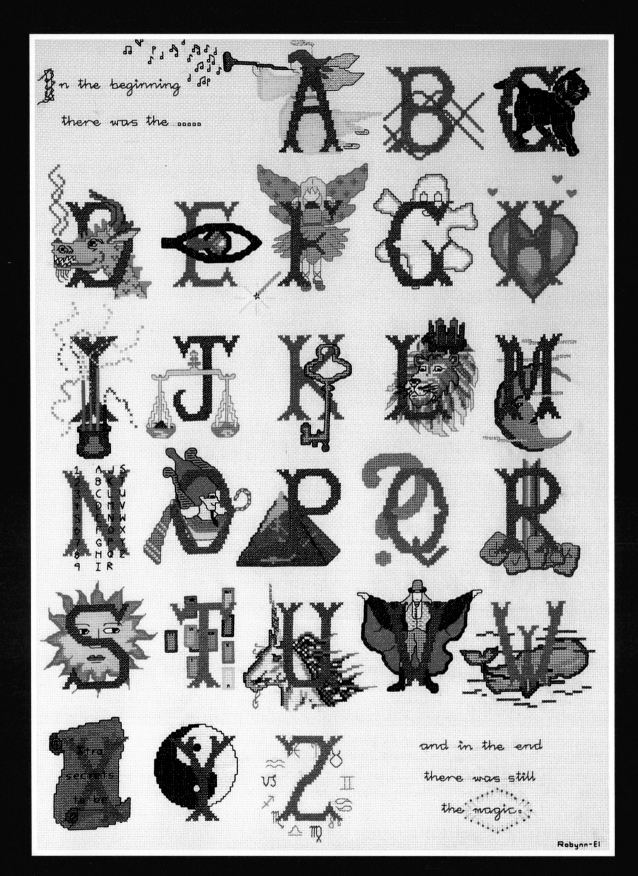

Steeds in Flight**

The finished design measures 37 cm wide by 34 cm high (14 ½" x 13 ½").

Fabric:
Cream Aida 14, approx. 47 cm x 44 cm (18 ½" x 17 ½") – you could choose pale pink, pale green or light blue Aida cloth instead of the cream, for a more dramatic effect.

Threads:

Symbol	DMC thread	Colour
••	745	pale yellow
Y	444	brilliant yellow
o	742	light orange
2	813	pale blue
Δ	996	light blue
B	995	intense blue
/	608	orange
r	666	red
D	816	dark red
3	913	light green
G	701	dark apple green
X	895	dark green
e	3609	pale pink
P	3607	pink
||	915	deep pink
✓	720	burnt orange
^	920	medium brown

Techniques used: *cross stitch and *overhand knots.

• Use 2 strands of thread for cross stitches.

Do all the cross stitching first so that the free-flowing manes and tails overlap the stitched bodies. This gives a three-dimensional effect.

Finishing
Use overhand knots to create the manes, tails and forelocks. Knot 3 lots of full 6-strand thread in stated colours, allowing only a little tail to remain at the back of the fabric. With a larger needle, thread it all to the front at the place marked on the graph with a black dot. (The knots stay on the wrong side of the fabric while the length of thread is pulled out front.) When you have finished threading for the whole mane or tail, brush all the threads up or out in the same direction, then

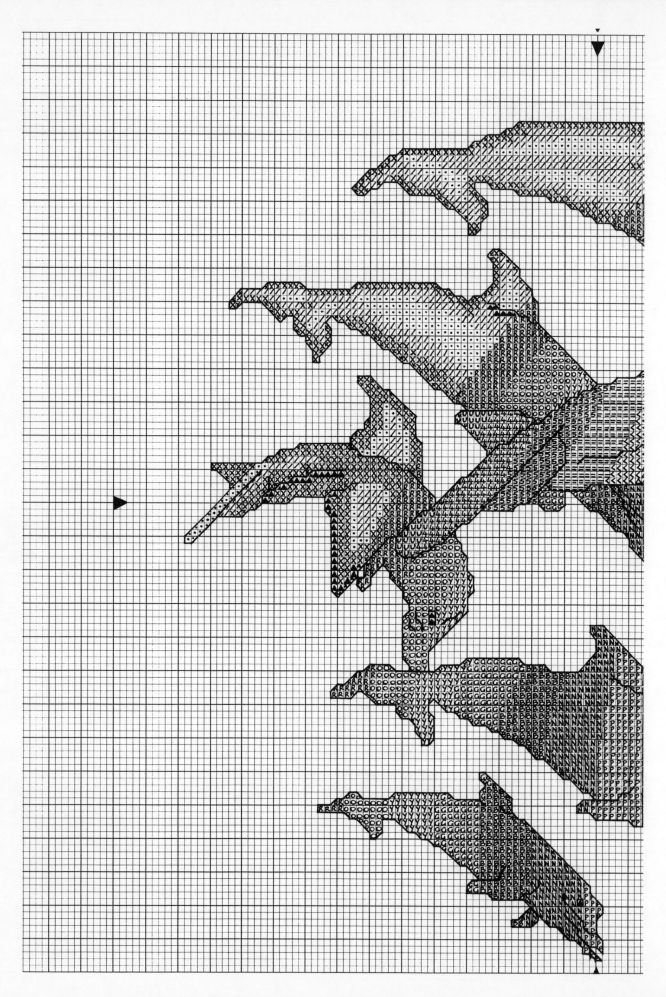

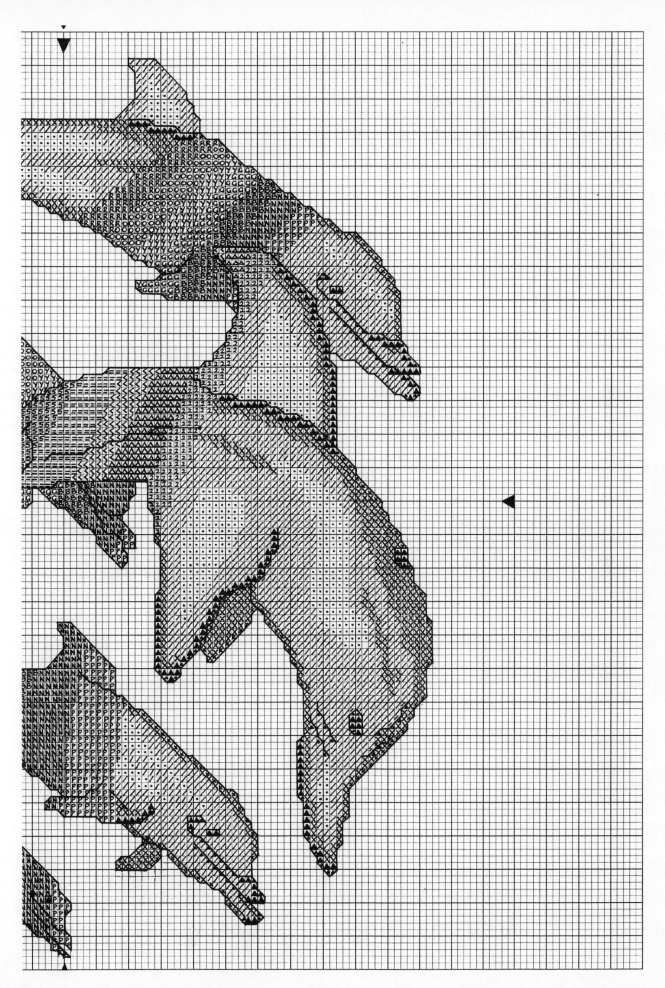

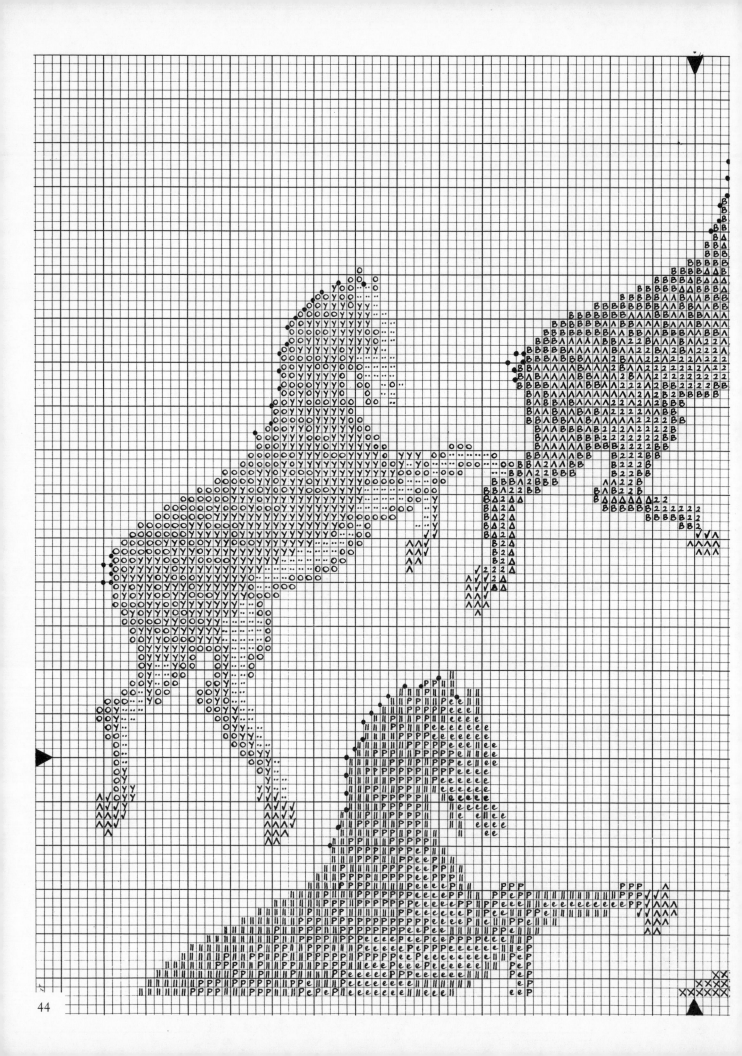

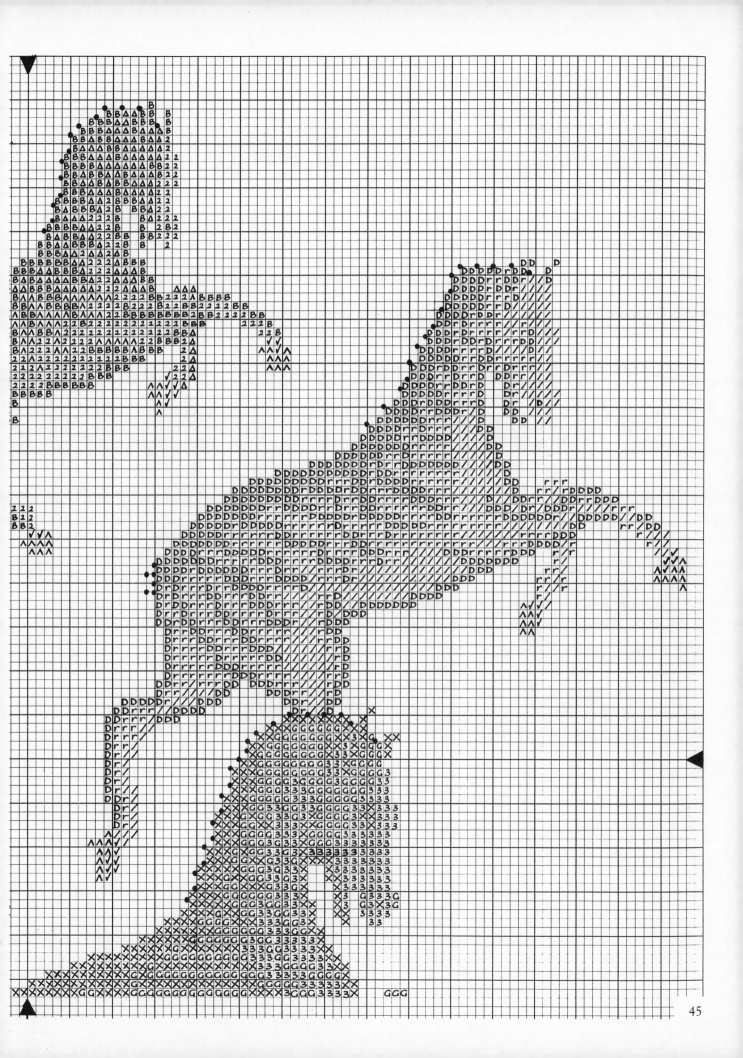

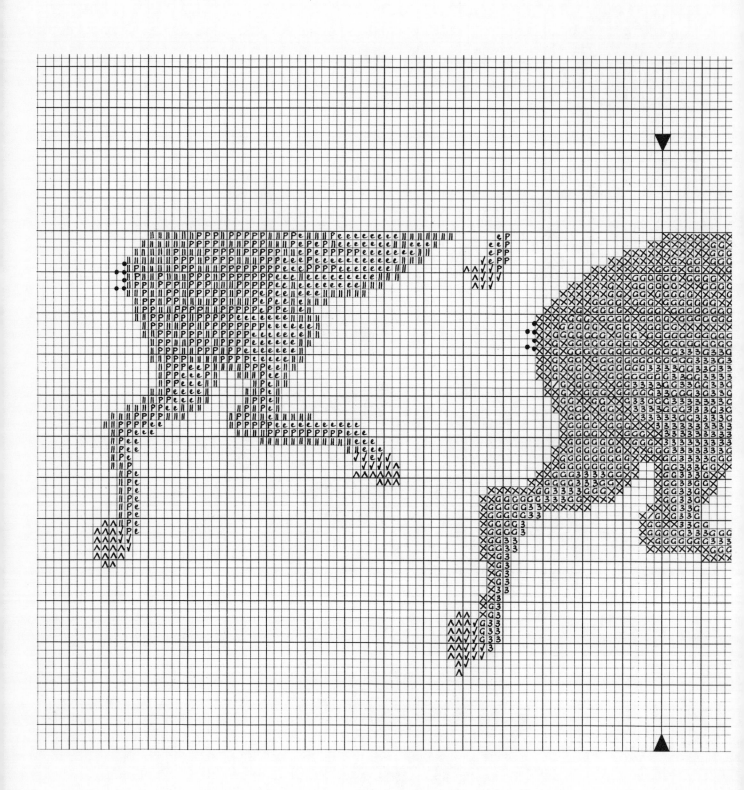

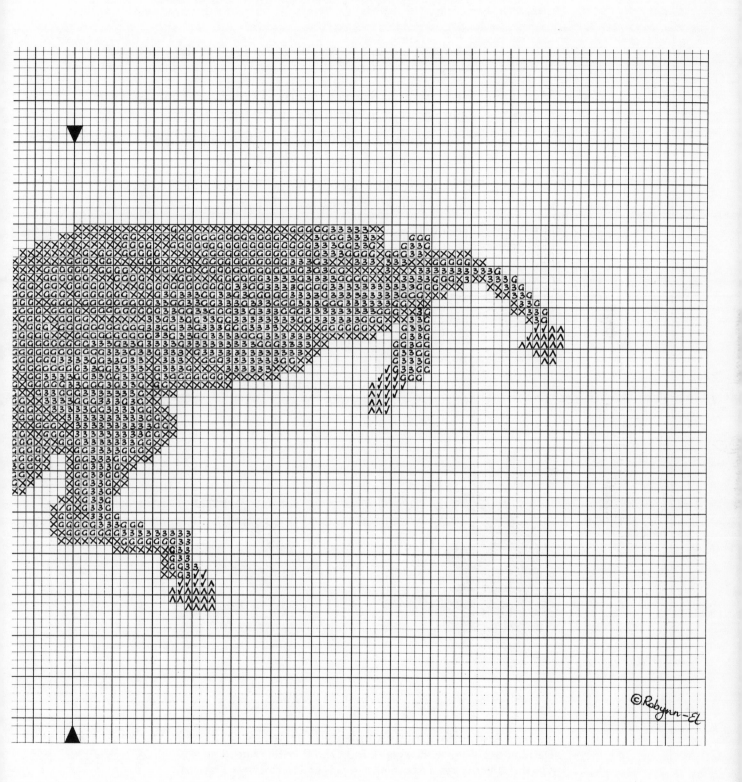

carefully trim them to the length as stated below.

Manes – cut to a length of 2.5 cm (1") at the front of the work.

Red horse: 11 knots using the 3 reds, plus 4 knots of the light and dark red with 996 blue.

Green horse: 16 knots using the 3 greens, plus 5 knots of the light and dark green with 666 red.

Pink horse: 11 knots using the 3 pinks, plus 4 knots of the light and dark pink with 701 green.

Yellow horse: 10 knots using the 3 yellows, plus 3 knots of the light and dark yellow with 3607 pink.

Blue horse: 10 knots using the 3 blues, plus 3 knots of the light and dark blue with 444 yellow.

Tails – cut to a length of 5 cm (2") at the front of the work. Use the same colour combinations as for the manes.

Red horse: 3 knots using the 3 reds, plus 3 of the light and dark red with 996 blue.

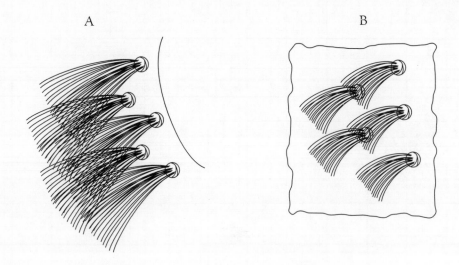

A   B

Attaching manes, tails and forelocks.
Detail of tail of horse showing A, front and B, wrong side of fabric.
(Overhand knot used for both manes, tails and forelocks *and* tassels)

Green horse: 3 knots using the 3 greens, plus 3 of the light and dark green with 666 red.

Pink horse: 3 knots using the 3 pinks, plus 3 of the light and dark pink with 701 green.

Yellow horse: 3 knots using the 3 yellows, plus 3 of the light and dark yellow with 3607 pink.

Blue horse: 3 knots using the 3 blues, plus 3 of the light and dark blue with 444 yellow.

Forelocks – cut to a length of 1.5 cm (⅝") at the front of the work.

For each horse, use 1 knot only for the forelock in the same colour combination as the mixed knot of the mane and tail on that same horse.

Mystical ABC ***

A   The angel represents your guardian spirit. With her halo, silver wings and slippers, she embodies kindness, purity and beauty.

B   Beginning at birth, each person's biorhythms indicate their physical, emotional and intellectual cycles. These three cycles coincide only once every 58 years.

C   If this curious black cat follows you, it means money. Its right paw in front symbolises the answer 'yes' to any question you may ask.

D   The mythical dragon peers through the D, ears alert, teeth bared, eyes never leaving his foe.

E   In The Book of the Dead, the Egyptian eye symbol was used at the end of a word to indicate its general meaning.

F   This little fairy does not realise she is supposed to be an imaginary supernatural being. She keeps popping into your life to show off her magical powers.

G   Being disembodied has not stopped this friendly ghost from smiling. If he isn't welcome, he just floats away on the next breeze.

H   The heart represents the life force, showing the depths of your conscience and emotions.

I   Incense is an aromatic substance burnt for its fragrant odour in religious ceremonies around the world.

J   Represented by the scales, justice is the moral principle that determines the fairness of our actions.

K   You need the key to unlock life's mysteries. When turned, it operates a mechanism so your pathway or mission in life may be revealed.

L   The lion embodies strength, courage and leadership. It is also a fire sign in the zodiac.

M   Silver clouds drift across the moon as the 'man in the moon' chuckles to himself upon hearing yet another superstition from mankind.

N   Numerology is the study of numbers and their supposed influence on human affairs. The Pythagorean alphabet is stitched here.

O   Osiris was the ancient Egyptian god who ruled the underworld and judged the dead.

P   Pyramid power has its roots in the ancient Egyptian royal tombs. Historians argue about construction, restoration, purpose and religious significance of these fantastic structures.

Q   The question mark denotes doubt about a subject. What is your quest in life?

R   Rainbows display all the colours of the spectrum. Spilling into Viking runes (showing separation, flow, the unknowable, movement and gateway), the rainbow gives them extra magical significance.

S   The sun is the star that is the source of heat and light for our solar system. Radiant warmth emanates from people with sunny dispositions.

T   Tarot cards made their first recorded appearance in medieval France in 1390 as an aid in fortune telling. The four suits of cups, swords, pentacles and wands are the ancestors of our modern hearts, spades, diamonds and clubs.

U   Legends say that the unicorn's spiral horn has a red tip, black mid-section and white base. The unicorn still roams the boundaries of your vision and your dreams and tosses his mane freely as he gallops back to his wilderness.

V   Tall, leggy and blonde, this vampire only preys upon thieves, murderers and vagabonds. Trapped in his immortal form, this is a vampire with a conscience.

W   Majestically powering through our oceans, whales have the support and love of millions of people in the world today.

X   'Xtra' secrets are revealed in the scroll when you are open, and willing to change and renew your philosophy of life. Are you ready for all the extras you can receive once this is accomplished?

Y   Yin and Yang are two complementary principles of Chinese philosophy. Yin is negative, dark and feminine. Yang is positive, bright and masculine. Harmony is maintained through their interaction.

Z   To predict your future astrology uses the circular diagram of the twelve signs of the zodiac, represented here in appropriate colour symbols to show earth, fire, water and air groups.

The finished design (the complete alphabet) measures 45 cm wide x 62 cm high (18" x 24 ½"). Each letter measures 6.3 cm high x 5- 5.8 cm wide, depending on the letter.

* The centre of each alphabet lies according to the overall space the design takes up, not the exact centre of the letter itself.

Fabric:
Cream Aida 14, approx 55cm x 70cm (22" x 28") for full alphabet or to size of individual letters. This size is finished dimensions, not allowing extra for mounting.

Threads:
1 skein each of the colours below should be sufficient to complete the alphabet.

Symbol	DMC thread	Colour	Letter
•	blanc	white	E, G, L, S, U, V, Y
z	208	dark mauve	F, L, R, T
3	211	light mauve	T
/	300	rich medium brown	P, Z
J	309	dark rich pink	D, T
▲	310	black	C, E, N, U, V
c	311	dark blue	G, M, W
o	318	blue grey	C, E, K, L, R, T, U, V, W, Y
h	335	deep pink	F, H, I, Q
↙	341	pale mauve blue	G, W
N	413	dark grey	P, T, W
Δ	434	light brown	T, X
8	444	brilliant yellow	F, L, R, S, V
⁞	445	bright lemon	J
■	498	burgundy red	H, L
Ø	501	grey green	I
2	550	rich purple	J, L, R, T
÷	553	light purple	Q, T
^	605	pale pink	C, L
U	606	tomato red	B, I, R, S, U
=	608	orange	A, C, D, I, P, R, T, Z
B	610	olive brown	A, I, L, T

||	632	medium brown	L, O
e	666	red	O, V
x	701	dark apple green	B, I, R
q	703	light green	I
M	720	burnt orange	J, L, S
▼	722	pale orange	P
K	725	mustard yellow	J, T
f	727	yellow	L, T
√	742	yolk yellow	A, D, S
5	801	dark brown	P, X
I	813	pale blue	M
a	819	hint of pink	A, F, O
L	893	pink	F, T
n	894	fairy floss pink	H, I, V
6	895	dark green	I, L, T
<	911	green	I, T
∩	918	rich brown	A, D, F, X
4	930	blue grey	K, R, U
+	958	jade	F, O, T, Z
\	959	light jade	F, T
>	973	bright yellow	A, O
*	995	intense blue	B, R, T, U
–	996	light blue	J, M, T, Z
w	3341	light salmon	D, T
7	3371	black brown	A, I
s	–	metallic silver	A, M
G	–	metallic gold	A, U

You will need 3 skeins of the following for the letters themselves:

g	699	emerald green	A, D, G, J, M, P, S, V, Y
b	796	royal blue	C, F, I, L, O, R, U, X
P	915	magenta	B, E, H, K, N, Q, T, W, Z

Techniques used: *cross stitch *three-quarter cross stitch *back stitch *French knots * tacking

Before stitching

On the graph I have made a grid as indicated by the horizontal and vertical lines of * * *. Carefully count and follow these lines with a tacking stitch in a pale-coloured cotton all over your Aida cloth. This method of dividing the overall design can save you time and possible errors later on. (It is frustrating when you are in the middle of a wonderful area of a design to find you are several squares out and need to undo the work and redo in the right space.) Naturally, you pull these guide lines out when you have completed your piece.

Threads and techniques for individual letters
* Use 2 strands of thread unless stated otherwise in individual letter instructions.

In the beginning there was the ...

- 2 strands of 796 for back stitching

- 2 strands of 699 for back stitching vines

- 2 strands of 915 for small French knots on ellipsis

A

Use 310, 608, 610, 699, 742, 819, 918, 973, 3371, gold, silver

- 1 strand of black for back stitching on wings and slippers

- 2 strands for back-stitched outlining everywhere else (e.g. 742 edge halo in gold; wings and slippers in silver)

- 3371 for back-stitched musical notes from trumpet and trumpet outline

B

Use 606, 701, 915, 995

- Outline every cross stitch of the biorhythm curve with 2 strands of same colour

C

Use 310, 318, 605, 608, 796

- 2 strands of black for outlining body

- 2 strands of 318 on body and whiskers

D

Use 309, 310, 605, 608, 699, 742, 918, 3341

- 2 strands of black for outline on mid-ear and mid-horns plus eye, nostril and teeth definitions

- 2 strands of 918 for outline on face, neck, ears and horns

- 2 strands of 608 for outline on scales

- 2 strands of 309 for smoke

- no outline on smoke or base of neck

E

Use 310, 318, 915, white

- 2 strands of white for outline on dot of eye

- 2 strands of black for outline everywhere else

F

Use 208, 444, 796, 819, 893, 918, 958, 959

- 1 strand of 918 for outline on face, hair, hands and legs

- 2 strands of 208 for outline on wings and belt

- 2 strands of 958 for outline on shoes and skirt

Sew on a gold star to end of pink wand with gold sparkles.

G

Use 311, 341, 699, white

- no stitching on eyes or mouth

- 2 strands of 311 for outline around positive and negative shapes

H

Use 335, 498, 894, 915

- 2 strands of 498 for outline around big heart

- 2 strands of 335 for outline around three little hearts

I

Use 335, 501, 606, 608, 610, 701, 703, 796, 894, 895, 911, 3371

- 2 strands of 895 for outline around pot

- 2 strands of self-colour outline around four incense sticks

- no outline on drifting smoke

J

Use 445, 550, 699, 720, 725, 996

- 2 strands of 720 for outline around bowls and handles of scales

- 2 strands of 550 and 966 for outline around same contents in bowls

K

Use 310, 318, 915, 930

- 2 strands of black for outline

L

Use 208, 310, 318, 444, 498, 550, 605, 610, 632, 720, 727, 796, 895, white

- 2 strands of black for outline around eyes, face, nose and whiskers

- 2 strands of 550 for outline around light and dark purple of crown

- 2 strands of 720 for outline around mane

- 2 strands of self-colour outline around crown and jewels on crown

- French knots on base of whiskers coming out of muzzle

M

Use 311, 699, 813, 996, silver

- 2 strands of 311 on left side of 311 cross stitch dark blue shadow and mouth

- 2 strands of 813 for lip division

- 2 strands of 966 on right side of moon and tips of shape

- 2 strands of silver for clouds and their outline

N

Use 310, 915

- 2 strands for back stitching of numbers and letters

O

Use 310, 632, 666, 796, 819, 958, 973

- 2 strands of black for outlining face, headgear and top

- 2 strands of 632 for outlining both royal standards

P

Use 300, 413, 608, 699, 722, 801

• 2 strands of 300 for outline on right edge of pyramid

• 2 strands of 413 for outline on lower left, base and right face of pyramid

• 2 strands of 722 for outline on tip of pyramid

Q

Use 335, 553, 915

• 2 strands of 335 for outline around 335 small question marks

• 2 strands of 553 for outline around 553 large question mark

R

Use 208, 318, 444, 550, 606, 608, 701, 796, 930, 995

• 2 strands of 208 for outline on right side of rainbow

• 2 strands of 606 for outline on left side of rainbow

• 2 strands of 930 for outlining runes and symbols

S

Use 310, 444, 606, 699, 720, 742, white

• 2 strands of black for outlining nose, lips and eyes

• 2 strands of 606 for outline on sunrays

T

Use 550 with 553, 610 with 434, 608 with 3341, 413 with 318, 958 with 959, 995 with 996, 208 with 211, 895 with 911, 309 with 893, 725 with 727, 915

• 2 strands of darkest colour for outlining each tarot card

• 2 strands of black for back stitching Roman numerals

U

Use 310, 318, 606, 796, 930, 995, white, gold

• 2 strands of black for outlining eye, nostrils, face and neck

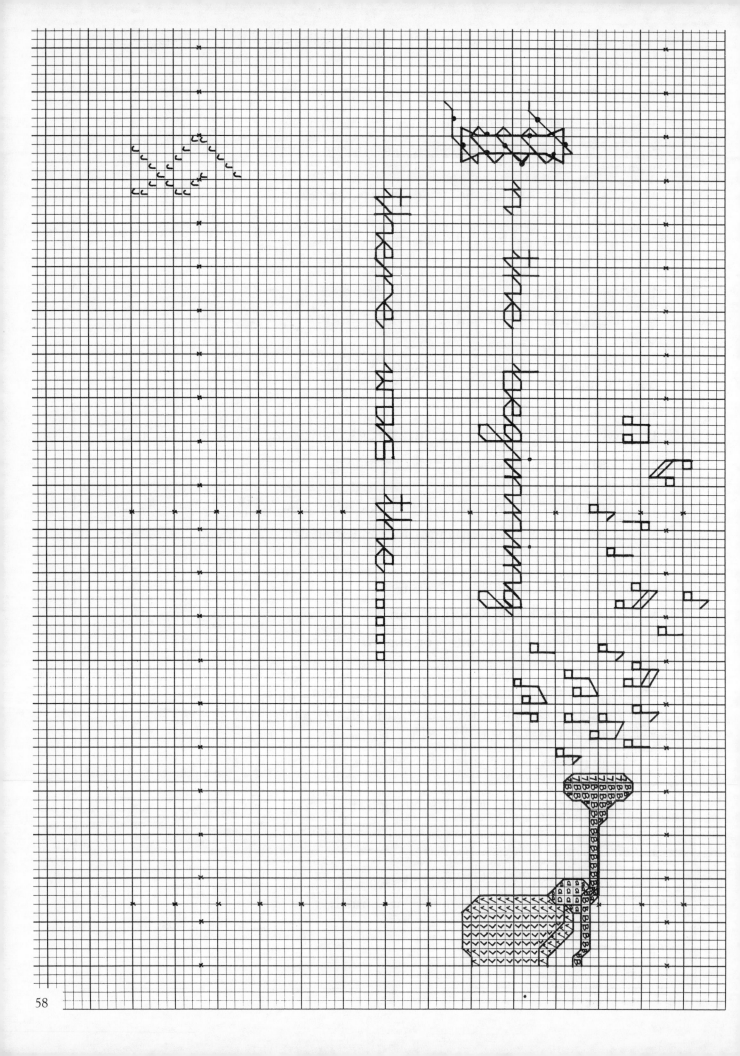

- 2 strands of 606 for outlining whiskers

- 2 strands of gold for long diagonal back stitch on tri-coloured horn

- no outline on mane to keep it free flowing

V

Use 310, 318, 444, 666, 699, 894, white

- 1 back stitch only in 666 for hint of mouth

- 2 strands of black for outline on cape, trousers, vest, buttons, hat, hair, hands, boots and shirt ruffle

W

Use 310, 311, 318, 341, 413, 915

- 2 strands of black for outline on body, eye, flipper and long bone

- no back stitch on waves

X

Use 310, 434, 796, 801, 918

- 2 strands of black for outline on scroll and back stitching words

Y

Use 310, 699, white

- 2 strands of black for outlining total shape, division of shape and both small circles

Z

Use 300 (earth), 608 (fire), 915, 958 (water), 996 (air),

- 2 strands for back stitching only

Note that the colour symbol is right next to the zodiac sign on the design.

and in the end there was still the magic

- 2 strands of 796 for back stitching

- 2 strands of 742 for sparkles

- 2 strands of 699 and 915 alternately for small French knots on end of sparkles (French knots also used as dots on the letters at the beginning and end of the design.)

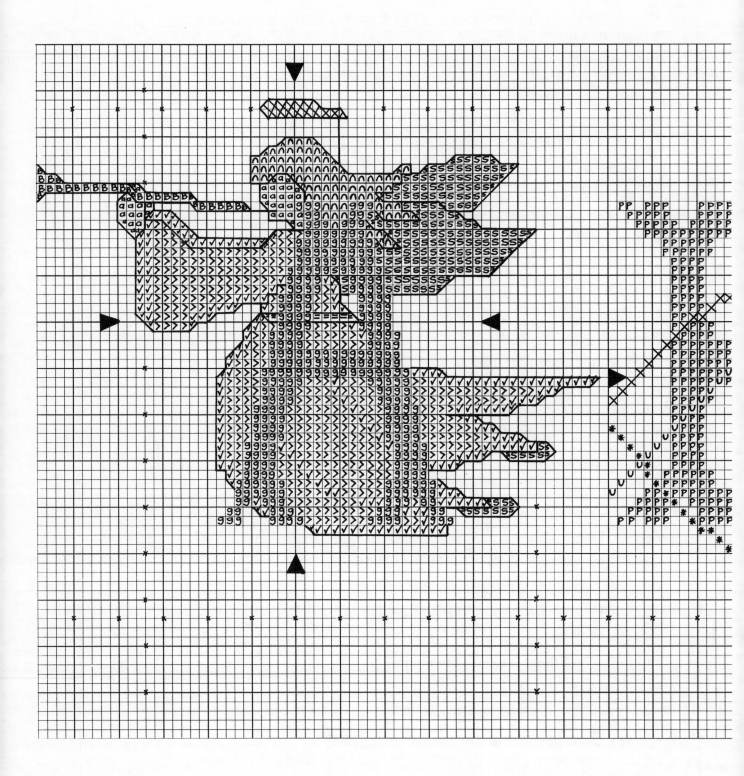

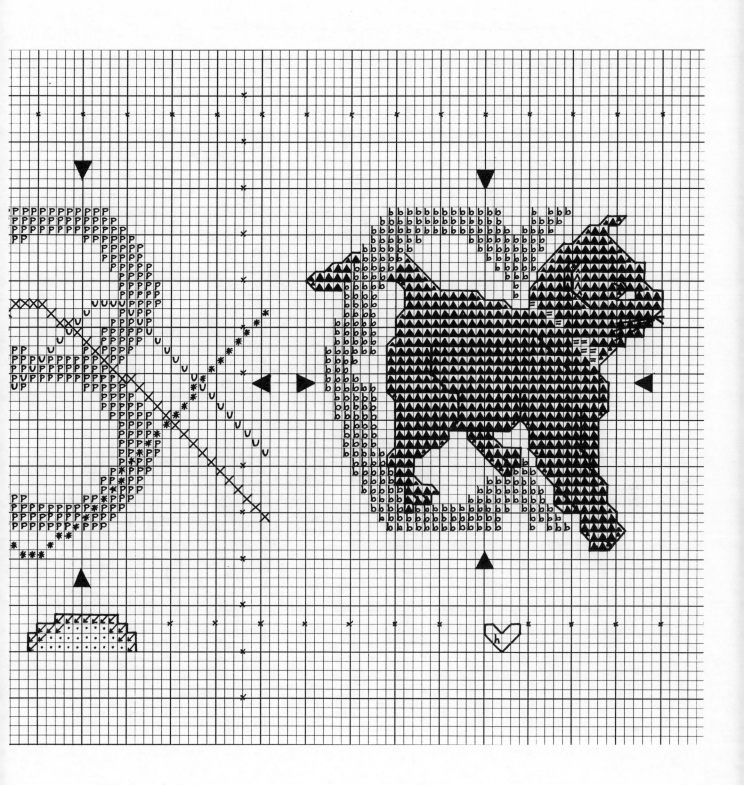

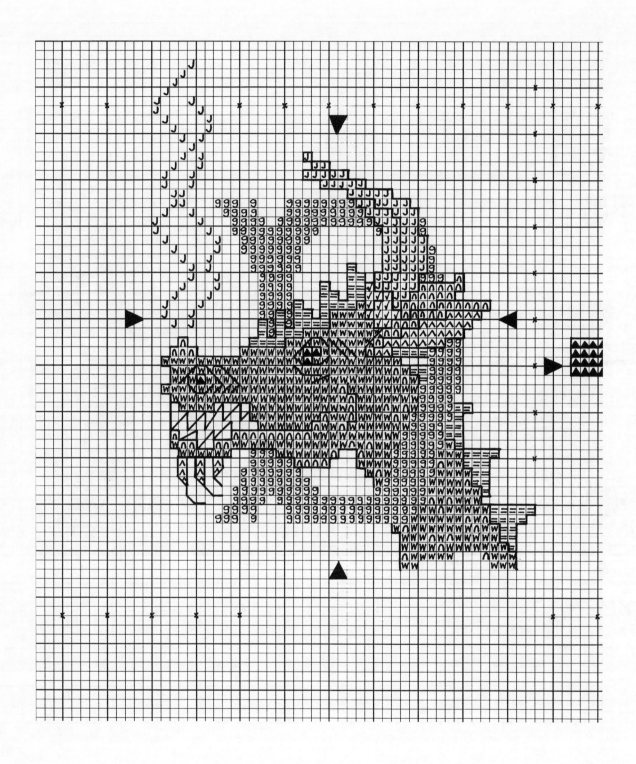

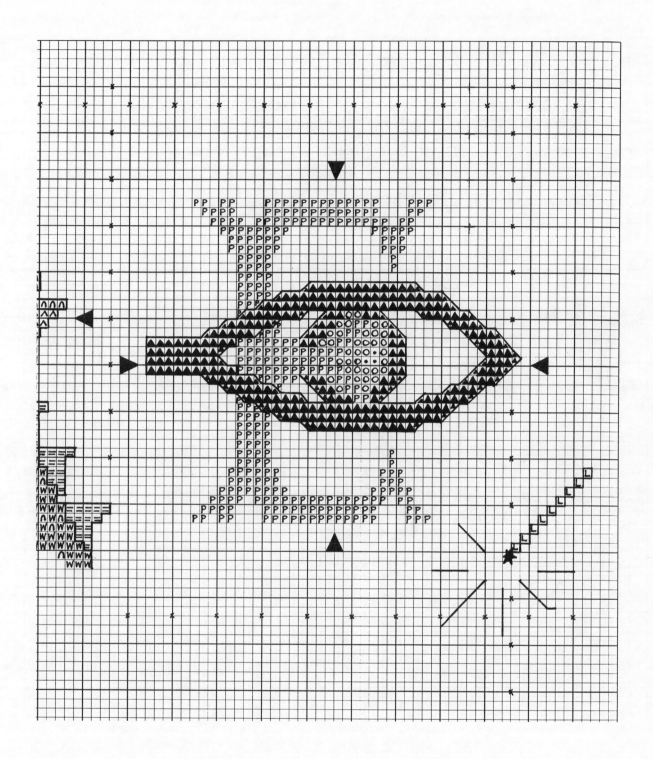

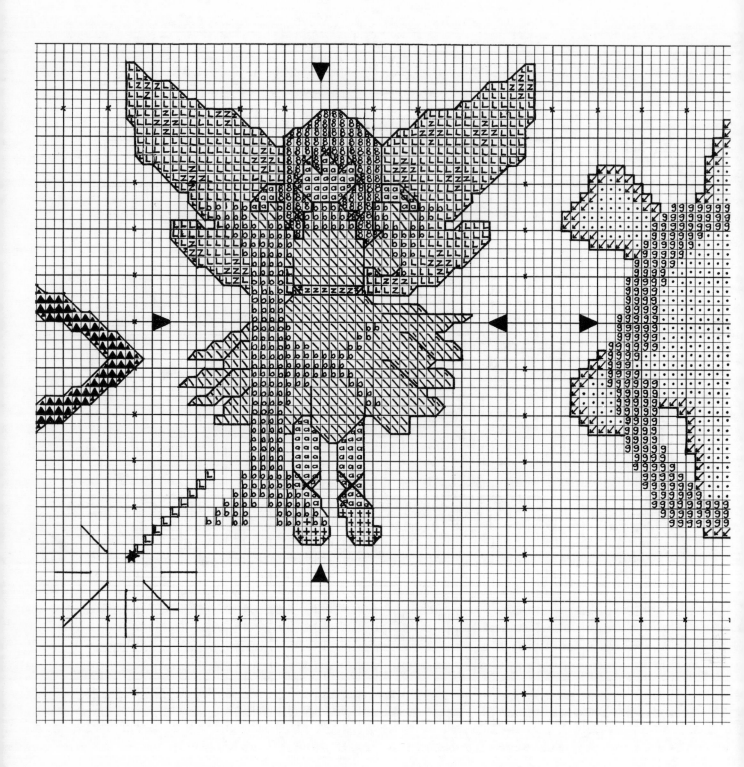

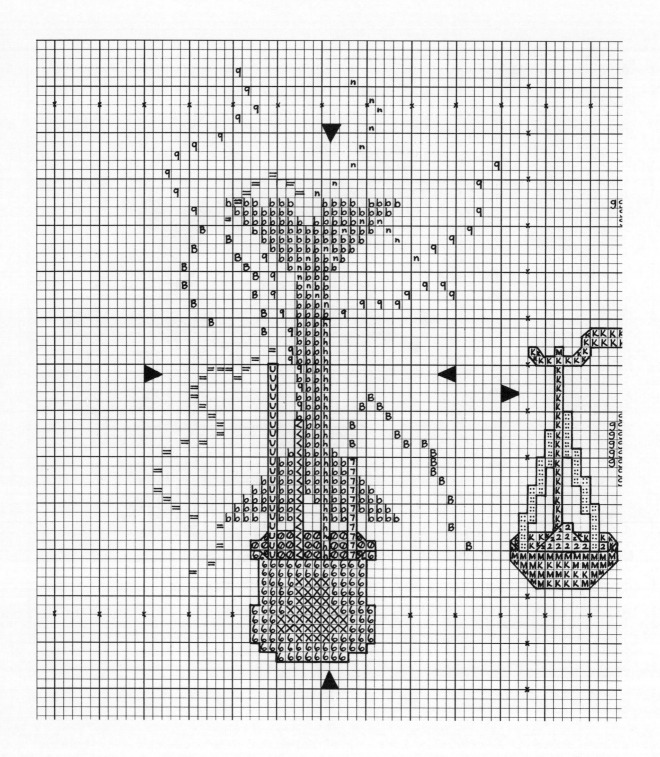

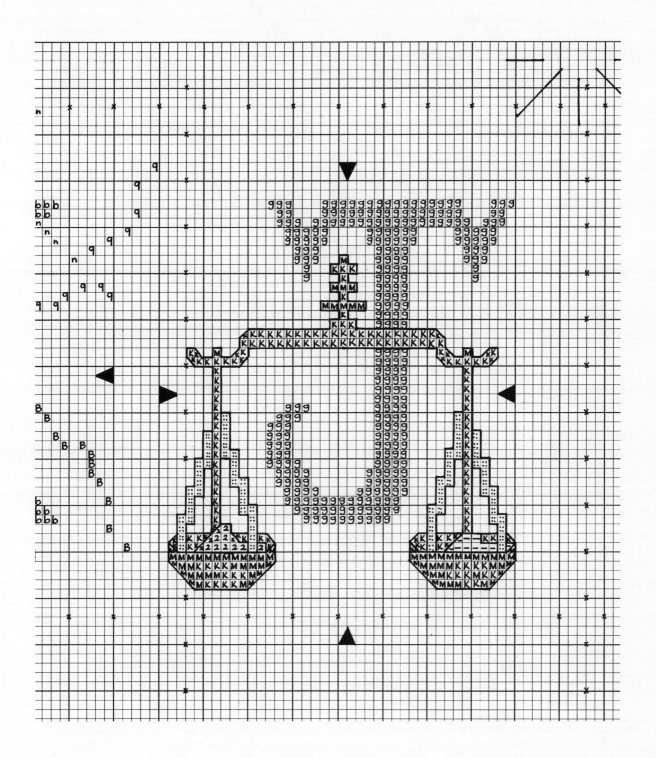

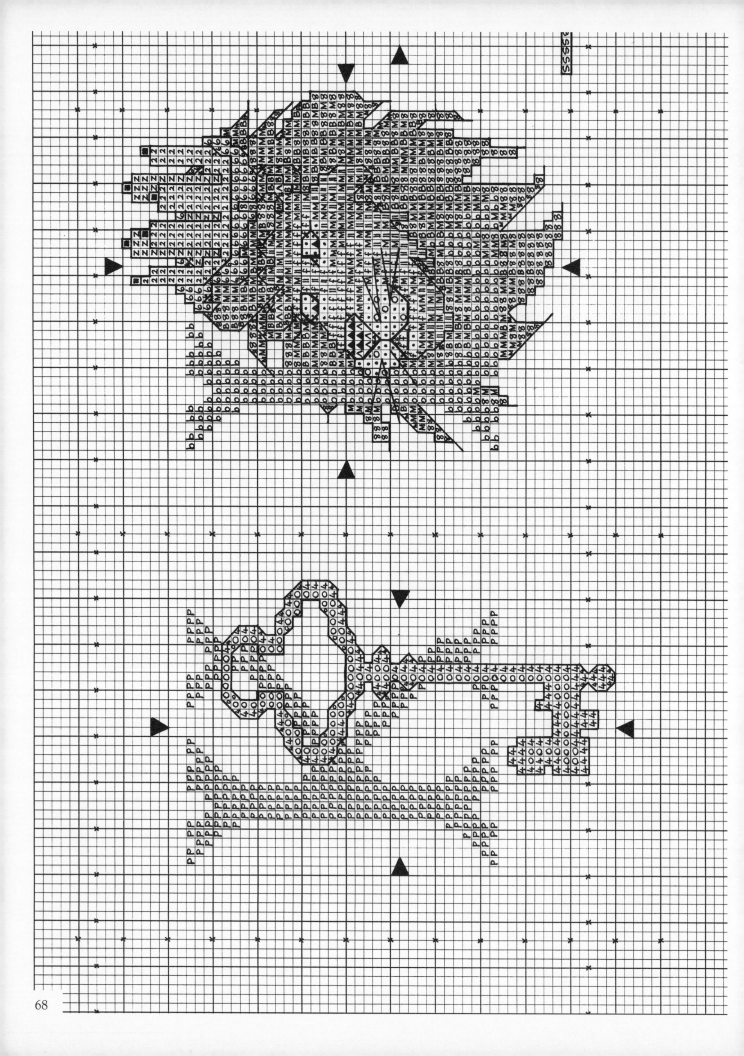

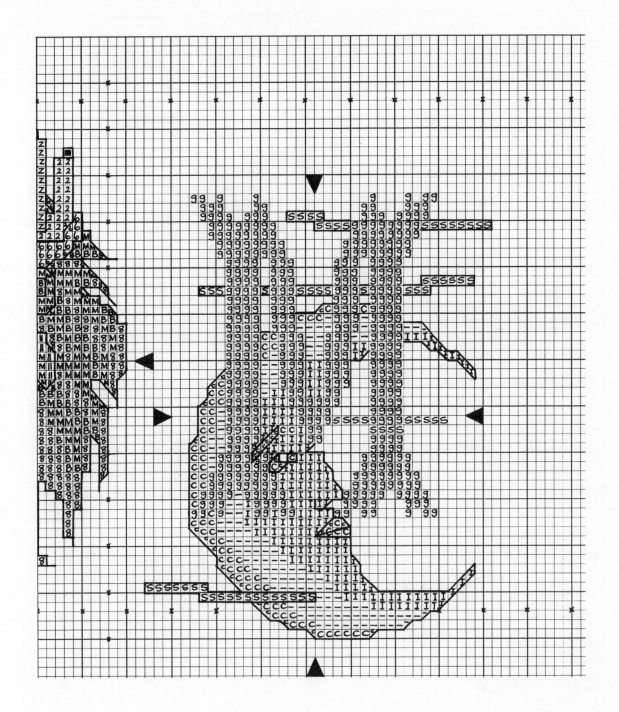

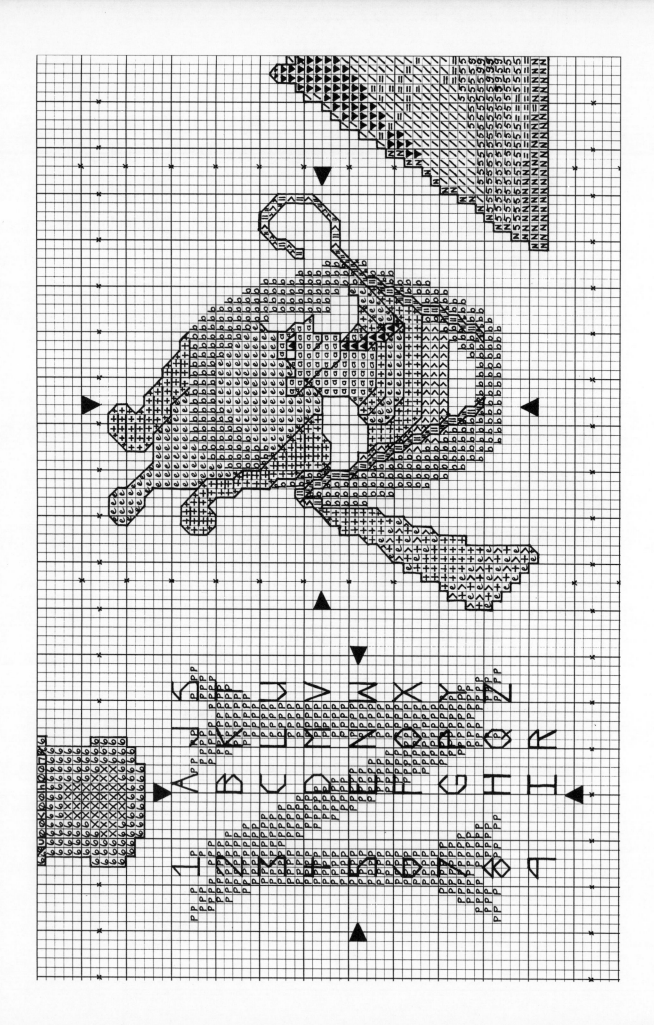

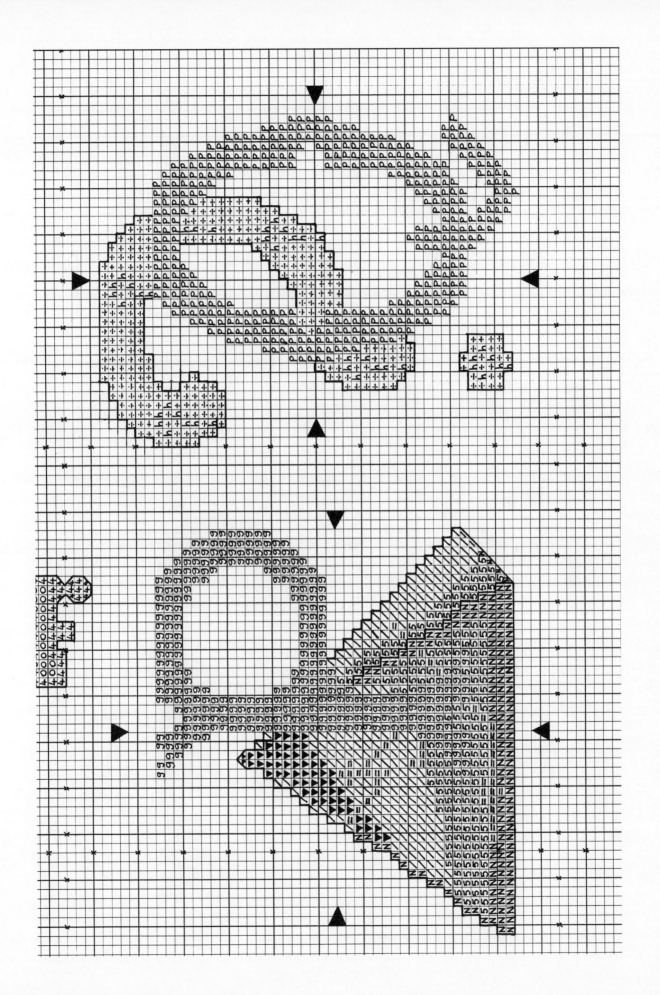

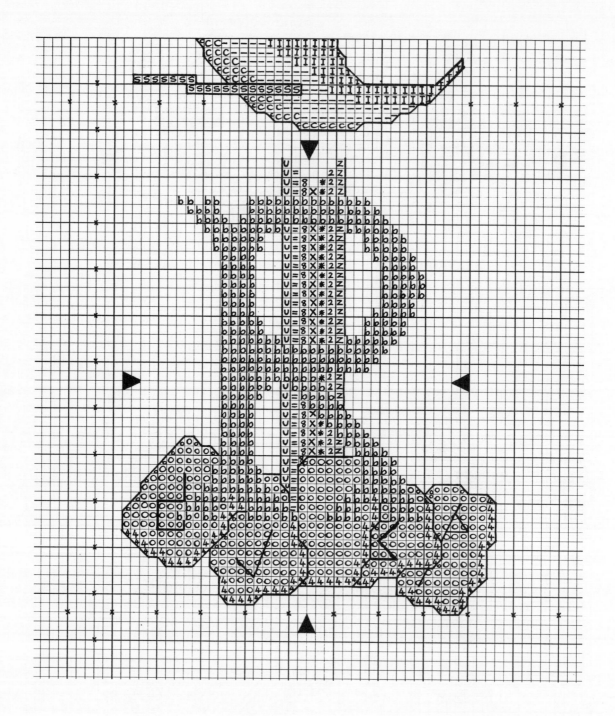

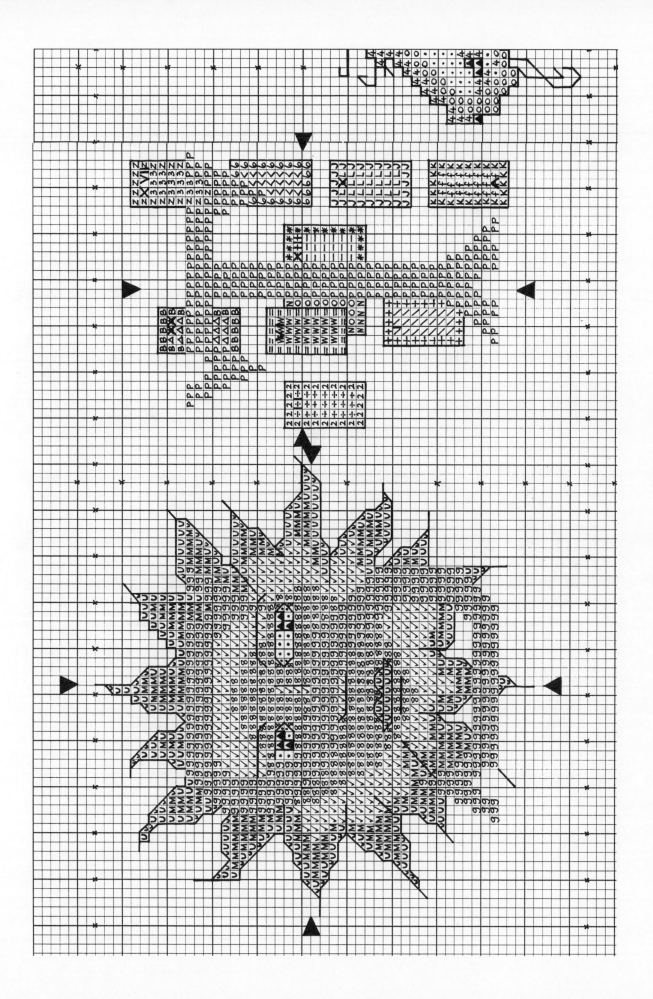

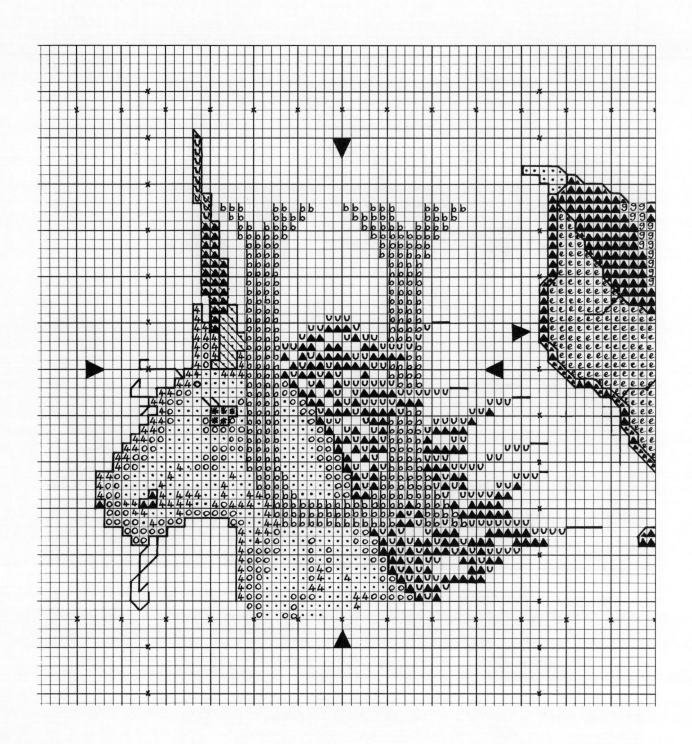

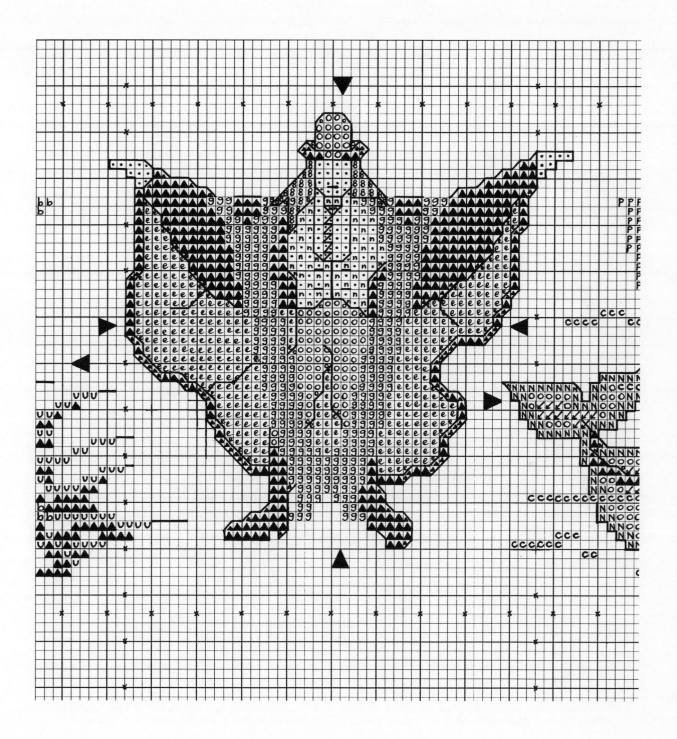

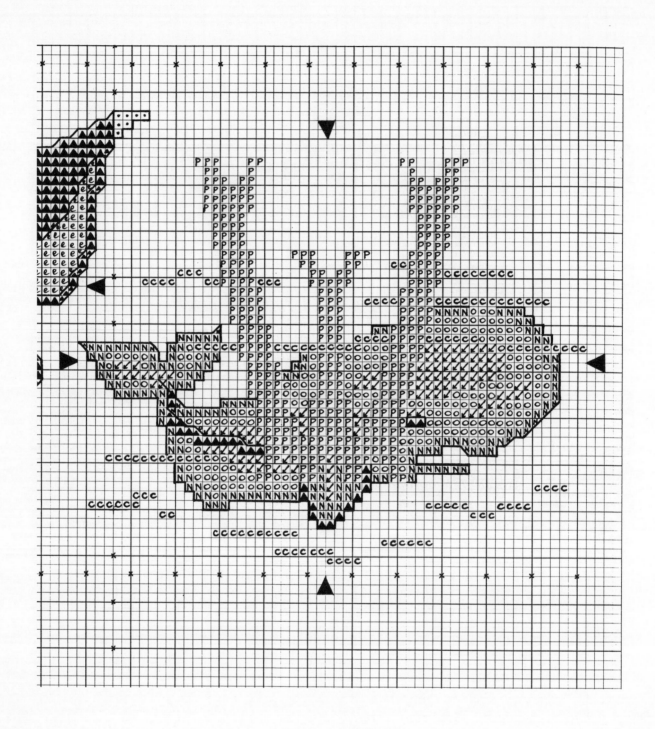

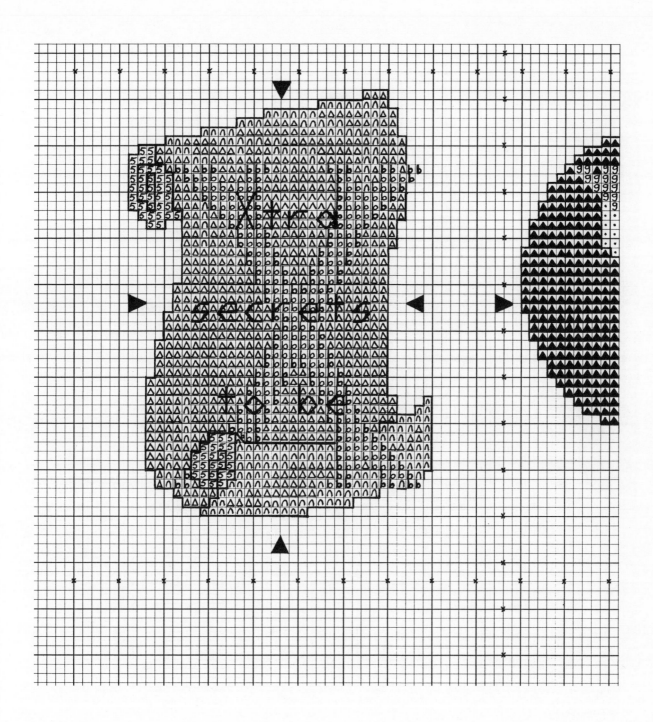

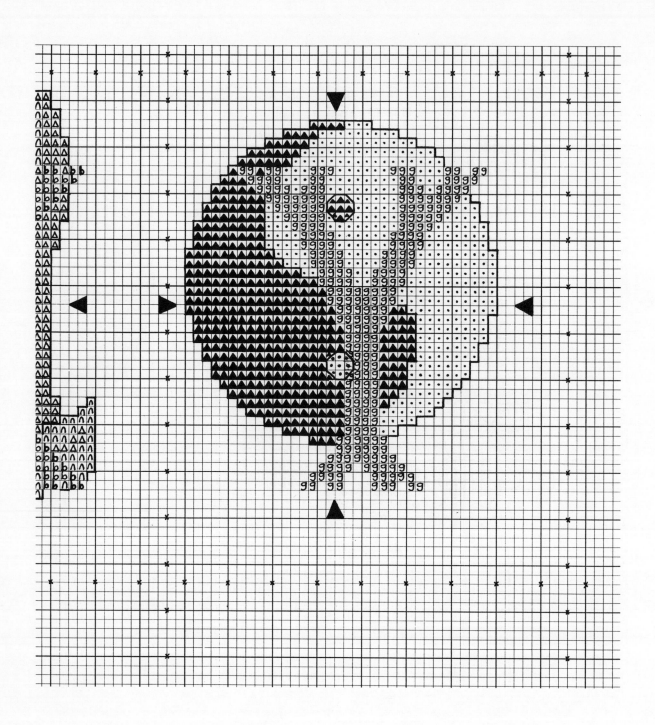

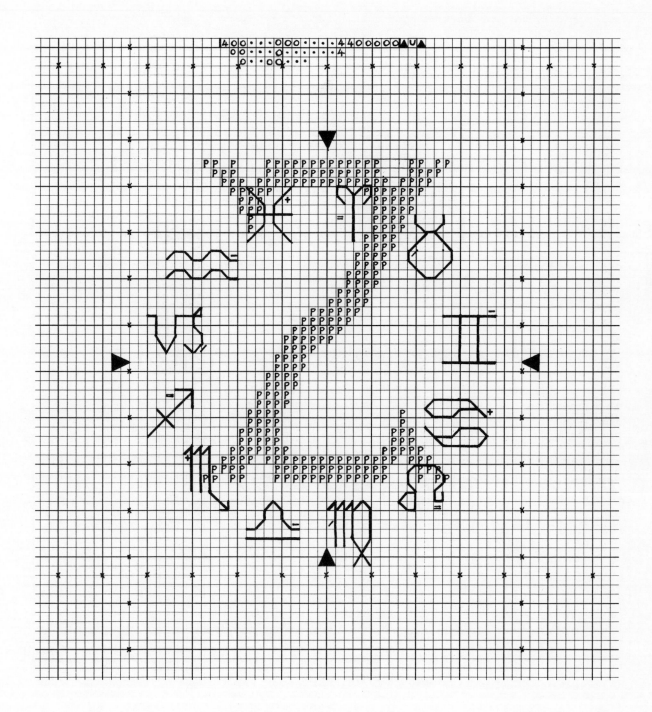

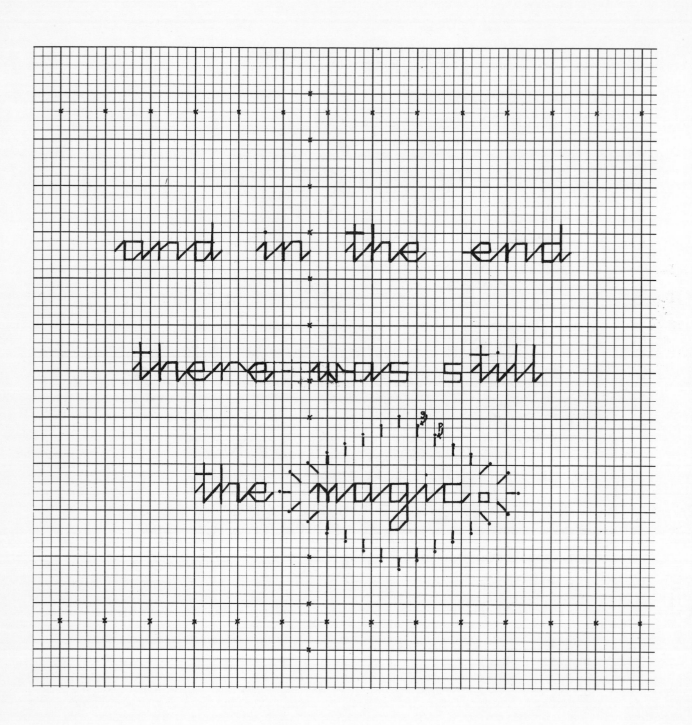

and in the end
there was still
the magic